HAUNTER OF RUINS

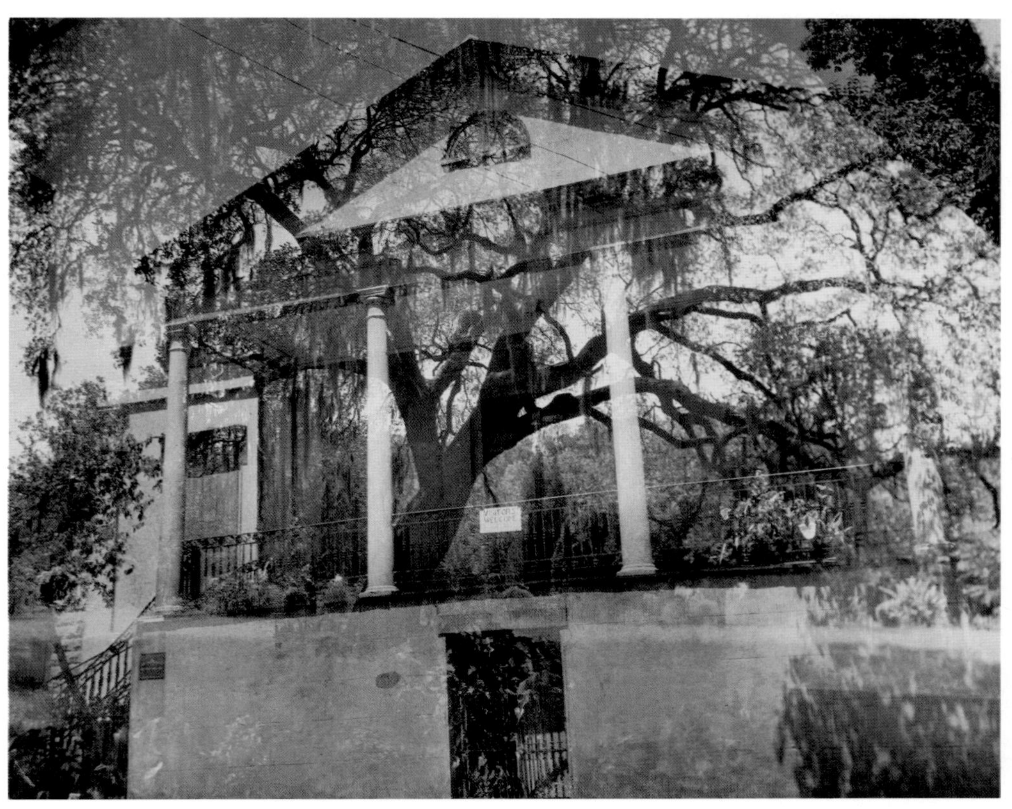

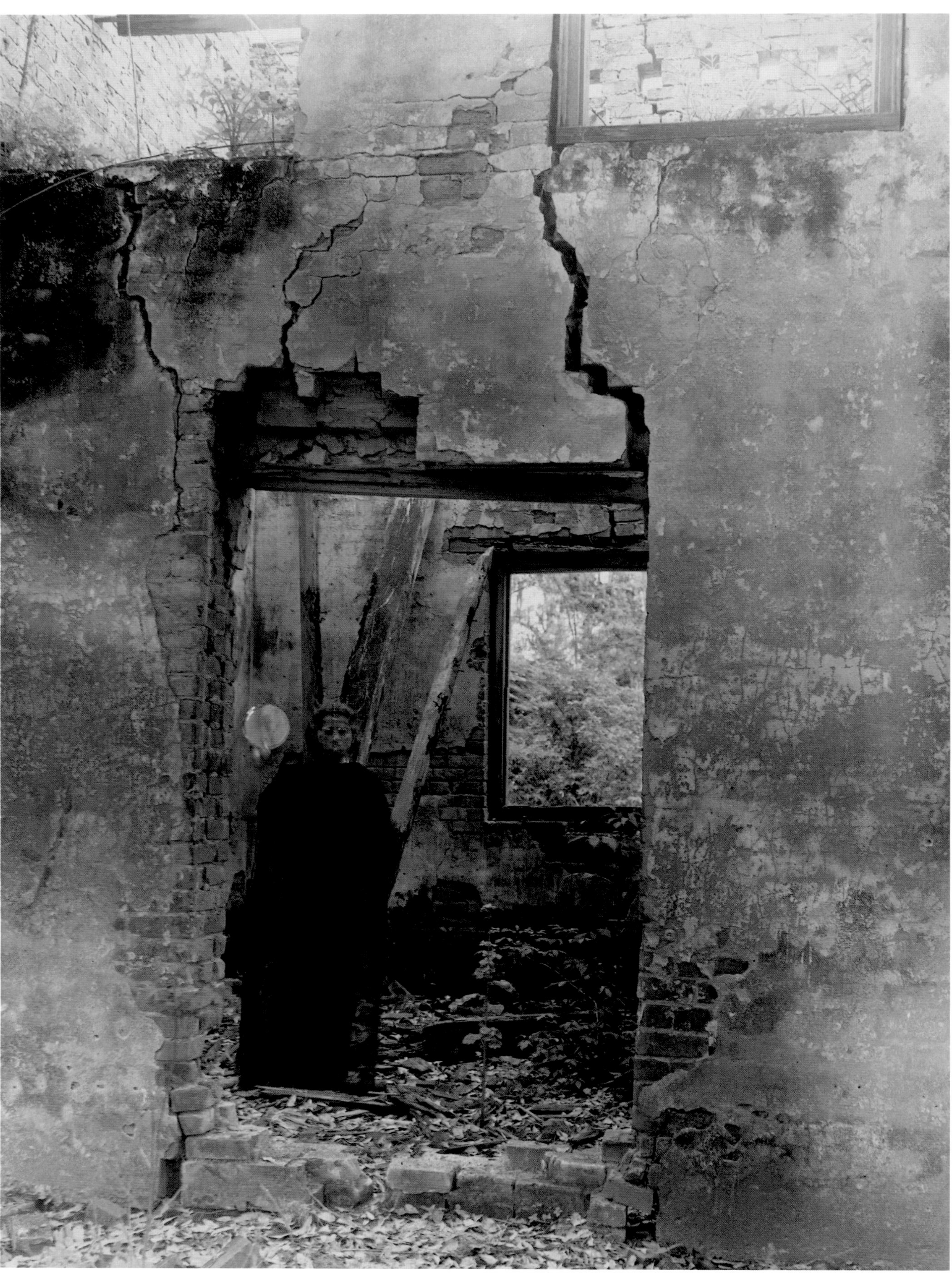

HAUNTER OF RUINS

THE PHOTOGRAPHY OF CLARENCE JOHN LAUGHLIN

Edited by John H. Lawrence and Patricia Brady
The Historic New Orleans Collection

With essays by Jon Kukla, John H. Lawrence, Andrei Codrescu, Ellen Gilchrist, Shirley Ann Grau, Jonathan Williams, Albert Belisle Davis, and John Wood

A BULFINCH PRESS BOOK
Little, Brown and Company
Boston New York Toronto London

Half title page: **THE BESIEGING WILDERNESS, NUMBER TWO,** *1938*

Joseph Cornell to Clarence John Laughlin, January 13, 1948
Nor have I forgotten the initial pleasure of seeing your work at ART OF THIS CENTURY evoking all kinds of wonderful things about what I dreamed about the South.

Frontispiece: **THE SEARCH FOR IDENTITY, NUMBER THREE,** *1941*

Man Ray to Clarence John Laughlin, April 29, 1941
There is no doubt that what you call symbolic use of the camera has not yet been exploited here [in the United States].

FIRST EDITION

The author is grateful for permission to include the following previously copyrighted material: Excerpt from *Les Fleurs du Mal* by Charles Baudelaire. Translation Copyright ©1982 by Richard Howard. Reprinted by permission of David R. Godine, Publisher.

Library of Congress Cataloging-in-Publication Data
Laughlin, Clarence John
Haunter of ruins : the photography of Clarence John Laughlin / edited by John H. Lawrence and Patricia Brady ; with essays by Jon Kukla . . . [et al.]. — 1st ed.
p. cm.
"A Bulfinch Press book."
ISBN 0-8212-2361-5
1. Photography, Artistic. 2. Cemeteries — Louisiana — New Orleans — Pictorial works. 3. Architectural photography — Louisiana — New Orleans. 4. Laughlin, Clarence John. I. Lawrence, John H. II. Brady, Patricia. III. Title.
TR654.L364 1997 97-4077
779'.092 — dc21

Bulfinch Press is an imprint and trademark of Little, Brown and Company (Inc.)
Published simultaneously in Canada by Little, Brown & Company (Canada) Limited

PRINTED IN ITALY

CONTENTS

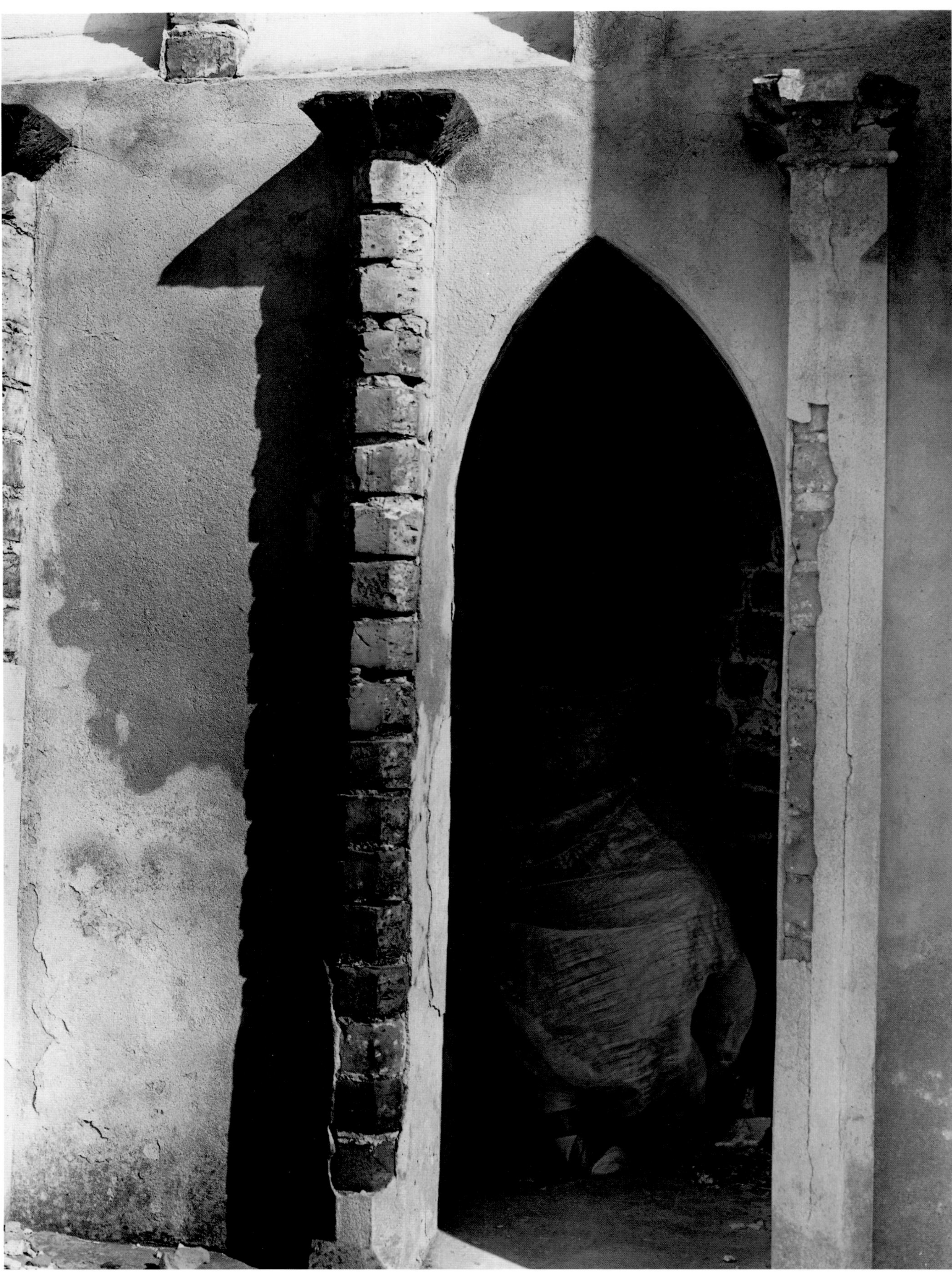

INTRODUCTION

The Wonder and Terror of Clarence John Laughlin

JON KUKLA

Since *Ghosts Along the Mississippi* first appeared in 1948, Clarence John Laughlin's photographic record of the vanishing plantation South has sustained an appreciative general audience through two dozen printings. For patrons and critics of twentieth-century art, Laughlin's photographs — especially his experiments with surrealism — place him in a distinct pantheon of American photographers. For his longtime friends, however, Laughlin is the subject of a favorite anecdote. As is often true of people with extraordinary talent, acquaintances find it easier to reminisce about eccentric mannerisms than to summarize the intensity of genius — and yet on closer examination the familiar story speaks to both.

Friends playfully suggest challenging the authenticity of a purported Laughlin photograph if it lacks the imprint of one of Clarence John Laughlin's shirt buttons pressed into its surface. Before he relinquished a photograph to the gaze of his visitor, the story continues, it was Laughlin's custom to clasp the print to his chest while exhorting the prospective viewer to a full anticipation of its merits. Despite the exaggeration that accompanies frequent repetition, this familiar tale of long and inescapable monologues about as-yet-unseen photographs hints at a truth that is implicit in this volume of his photographs published with commentary by Laughlin and a distinguished company of authors.

Clarence John Laughlin routinely presented his clients with a picture and at least a thousand words, but in his book-lined attic studio in the Upper Pontalba Building, the words came first. Words had come first in Laughlin's career, too, and his linking of image and text was never erased. Authorship both frustrated and fascinated Laughlin. For anyone whose mind perceives more complexity than can be expressed on a bumper sticker or in a sound bite on the evening news, the challenge is to create a single linear text, choosing and placing each letter and each word to march in an orderly sequence across one page and onto the next. Words set carefully in this fashion invite a reader to follow the line of letters, decipher the linear sequence of words, and re-create in one's consciousness an approximation of the full complexity originally perceived in the mind of the author.

Opposite:
FIGURE IN A CRYPT
1940 or 1941

Weeks Hall to Clarence John Laughlin, December 1, 1943

I also saw that you were Celtic and that the existent world is mere symbol to you. You feel that the way to see things is to see around them rather than to touch them.

It was difficult enough for Laughlin's multiple genius to compress a three-dimensional universe onto the flat plane of a photographic image. Driven to extend "the individual object into a larger and more significant reality,"[1] Laughlin's imagination invested meaning in the black-and-white patterns left by millions of subatomic particles of light organized by his lens, released by his shutter, and sent crashing toward the surface of his photographic negatives. Then, Laughlin often applied layers of words to point viewers toward his dimensions of meaning and truth. In short, Clarence John Laughlin found in photography a medium with which to proclaim his visions, long after his studio fell silent and the surfaces of his master prints had relinquished the temporary impressions of his shirt buttons.

"Photography," Laughlin wrote, "is one of the most authentic and integral modes of expression possible in this world in which we live."[2] Had this comment about photography been destined for publication during his lifetime, no doubt a quick-thinking editor might, at first glance, have raised a blue pencil to delete the last several words. Then, reflecting further about *this world in which we live,* a thoughtful editor would have let them stand. Phrases like this, found throughout Laughlin's correspondence and unpublished essays, are a clue to the nature of his visions and of his art. Clarence John Laughlin was deeply troubled by the emerging nature of a modern world in which the responsibilities of mind were being overtaken by a civilization of machines. In ways that were both characteristic of universal mid-twentieth-century human experience and highlighted by the situation of his New Orleans, Laughlin found it profoundly disturbing that humanity was being "shoved onto a plane on which the screw, the gear, and the girder reign."[3]

More than aesthetic taste was at issue when Laughlin reacted strongly against the "'soft focus' approach . . . of balcony and courtyard scenes by the arty professional French Quarter photographers"[4] — best exemplified by his contemporary Eugene Delcroix. At the time, New Orleans itself was being physically altered by gargantuan devices aimed at controlling and exploiting the Mississippi River. Bridges, wharves, and floodgates built to contend with the Mississippi are mammoth beyond the scale of their counterparts in all but a few cities in the world. Upriver and down, rows of gingerbread-bedecked shotgun houses following the curves of the river now share their narrow streets with enormous steel towers, their bases wider in diameter than two-hundred-year-old oaks, carrying electricity through metal cables as thick as a man's arm. The accelerating mechanization of life engulfed Laughlin and his international contemporaries, but in New Orleans its huge devices of peacetime modernity were (and are) juxtaposed against the ancient human dimensions of a colonial and Victorian city standing on such a deep accumulation of river silt that skyscrapers of more than four hundred feet awaited the second half of this century.

The Laughlin who roared at "these same French Quarter men" and

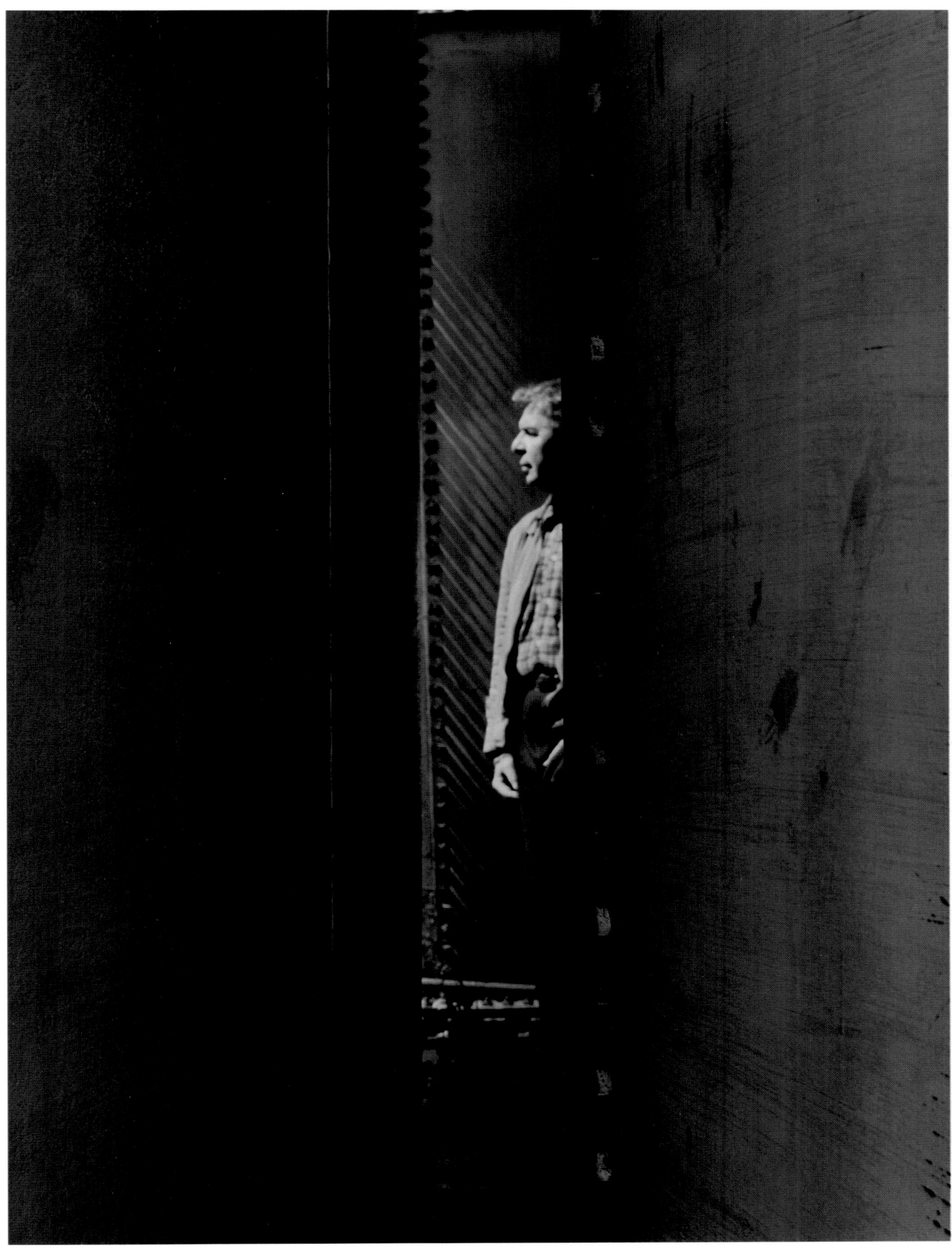

CLARENCE JOHN LAUGHLIN, *1956*

Photoprint by Larry Colwell

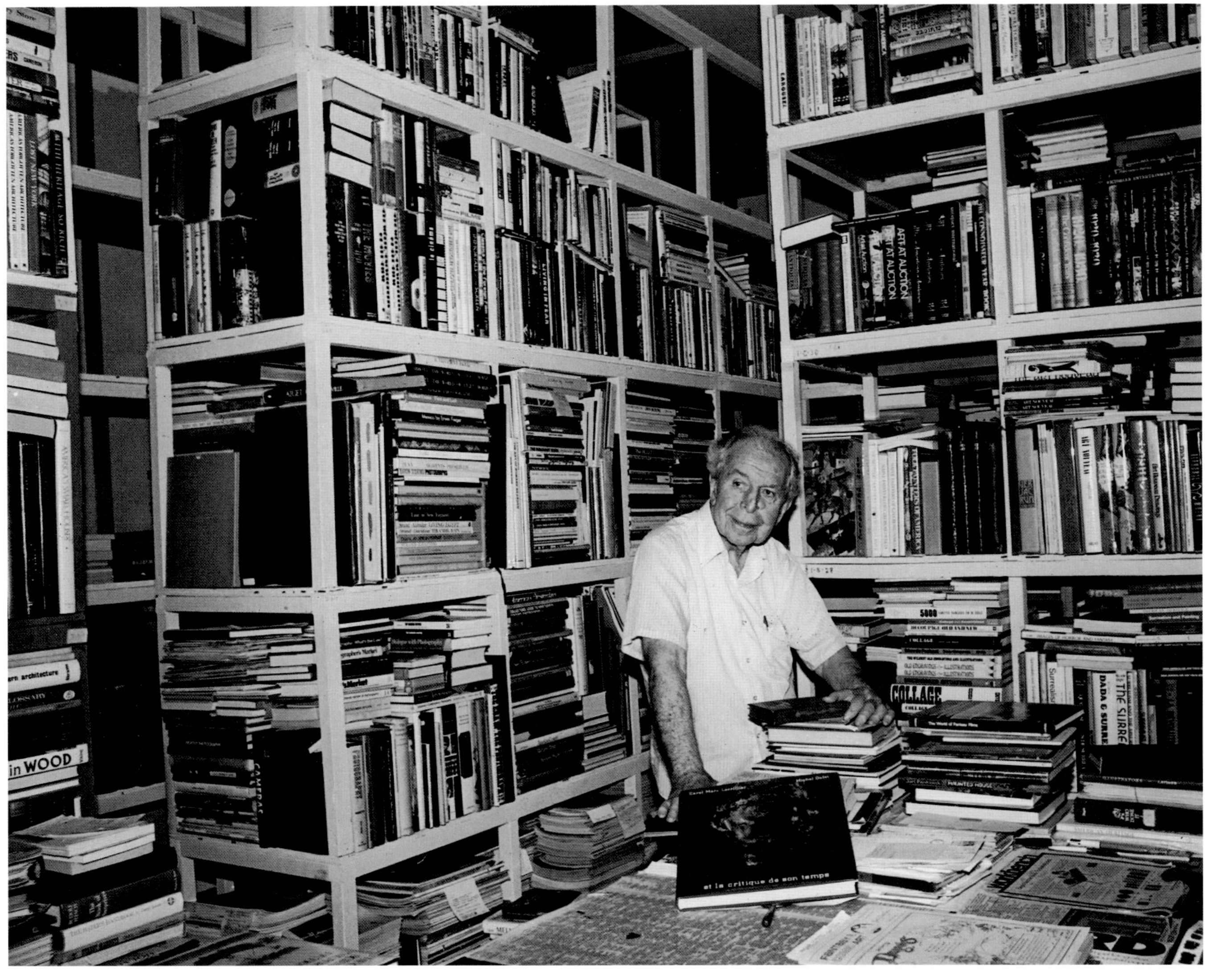

CLARENCE JOHN LAUGHLIN IN HIS LIBRARY
1981

Photoprint by Nancy R. Moss; gift of Mrs. P. Roussel Norman

their arbitrary division of "reality into so-called 'beautiful' and 'ugly' objects" was gracious to acknowledge that rejecting their selective nostalgia had forced him to confront his own central themes: Laughlin refused to look away from "the wonder and terror of our times."[5] Rather, looking with a poet's eye at the sights and experience of his city and its environs, he found in it the exemplar of a modernity "in which the present and the past discordantly mingled."[6] Although itself a device prone to misuse, "the camera is a machine only when it is used mechanically."[7] Laughlin felt that, employed with imagination, the camera could at least help us see "the steel magic of . . . misdirected machinery" and "the mad clockwork tragedy of it all."[8]

Preserved in his vast archive at the Historic New Orleans Collection is a long and revealing letter that thirty-one-year-old Laughlin sent to Margaret Bourke-White with sixteen photographs in July 1936. After "working in the business world, mostly in banks," since 1920, he had "rebelled against the[se] values and rituals" and was contemplating his future. As Laughlin described his hopes to Bourke-White, we now can see that his road not taken was paved with words: an unfinished novel whose "central figure is a *clerk,* who is acted upon by all the things and situations peculiar only to our era," as well as being "a symbol summing up the total plight of man in the modern world."[9]

The world was spared a Depression-era version of *Bartleby the Scrivener,* but Laughlin's letter to Bourke-White also presaged the road he *did* travel. Characteristically, in light of his subsequent accomplishments, Laughlin was already assigning his photographs to thematic series. In 1936 he spoke of figure studies and portraits; symbols of old New Orleans; still lifes, marine and plant forms; "visual experiments" and "the minatory beauty of machinery"; and "a composite print from two negatives" from a series, he told Bourke-White, "on which I intend to work a great deal more . . . with the possibilities of social and philosophical ideas in photography."[10] Half a century later, by his death in 1985, the thematic photographic series represented in this volume were more numerous and sophisticated — worthy visual subjects for the writers whose essays have been commissioned for this collection — for Clarence John Laughlin had proved his genius not as a latter-day Melville at the typewriter but rather as an Edgar Allan Poe with a camera.

Notes

1. Clarence John Laughlin, "Some Observations on the Functions of Photography" (1939), Clarence John Laughlin Collection, The Historic New Orleans Collection, 8.
2. Ibid.
3. Clarence John Laughlin, "A Statement," n.d., Clarence John Laughlin Collection, The Historic New Orleans Collection, 2.
4. Laughlin, "Some Observations," 5; "A Statement," 2.
5. Laughlin, "Some Observations," 5.
6. Ibid.
7. Clarence John Laughlin, *Ghosts Along the Mississippi: An Essay in the Poetic Interpretation of Louisiana's Plantation Architecture* (New York: Scribner's, 1948), xv. "Photography in America," Laughlin also commented, "suffers from a plethora of equipment and gadgets, an overabundance of technical proficiency, and a dearth of actual achievement." (Unpublished essay, n.d., Clarence John Laughlin Collection, The Historic New Orleans Collection, 8.)
8. Laughlin, "A Statement," 2.
9. Clarence John Laughlin to Margaret Bourke-White, July 21, 1936, Clarence John Laughlin Collection, The Historic New Orleans Collection.
10. Ibid.

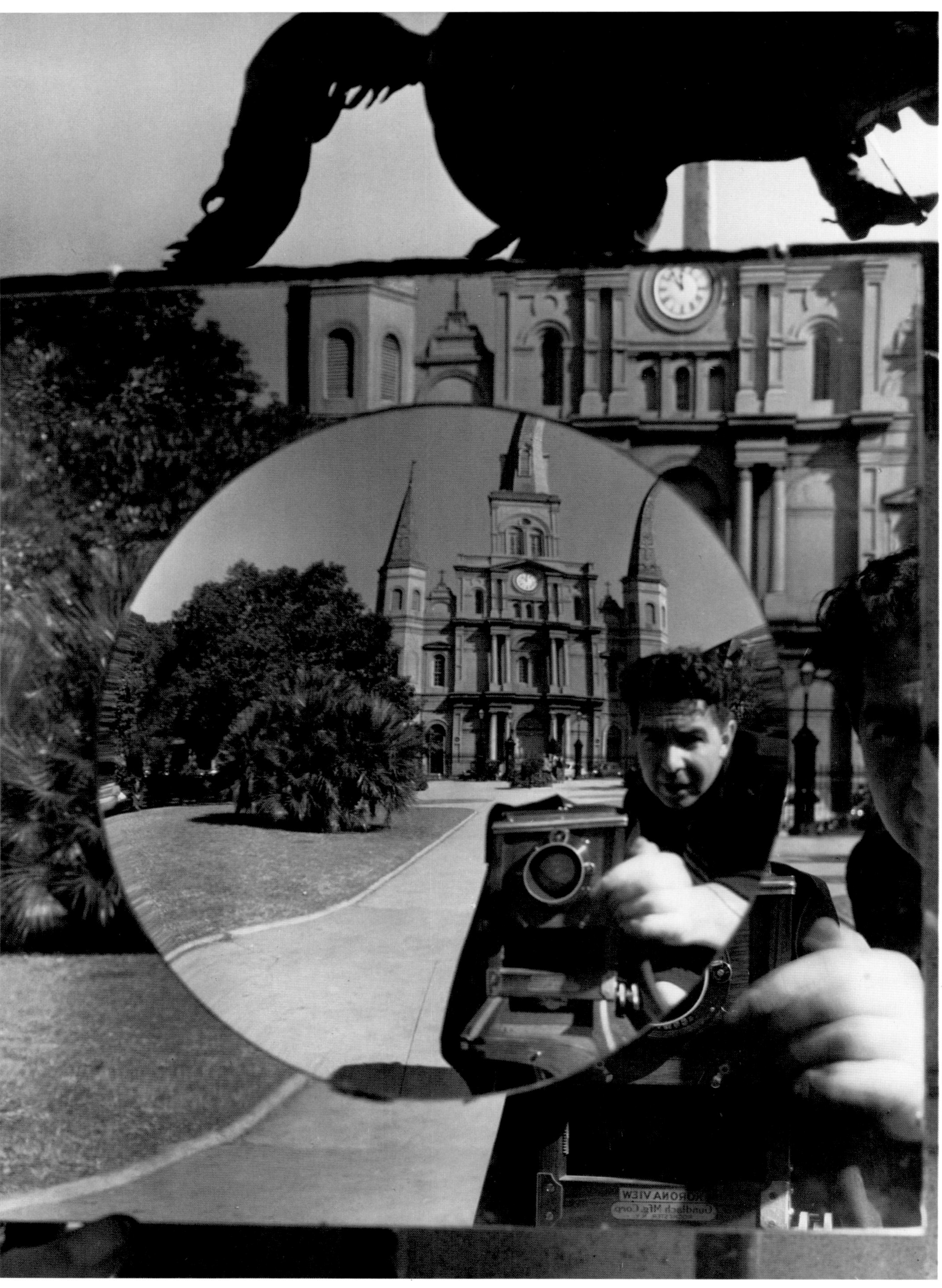
KORONA VIEW
Gundlach Mfg. Corp

Images and Words

JOHN H. LAWRENCE

Opposite:
PORTRAIT OF THE PHOTOGRAPHER AS A METAPHYSICIAN
1941

"Architecture and the Camera" (August 1949), typescript

My gradually evolved conviction that the camera could be used as an instrument to explore the mind of man, the inner world where man lives both by symbols and emotions, and that in achieving this, the camera would have been used in such a way that it became a direct extension of the luminous and super-sentient eye of the imagination — a third eye!

At his death on January 2, 1985, Clarence Laughlin remained, like the title of one of his best-known photographs, an enigma. Labeling him as such is no more or less accurate or useful than calling him a surrealist, a romantic, a modernist, or a fantasist, though each of these terms describes an aspect of Laughlin's character and his achievements as a visual artist. To explain the mystery of Laughlin's work would be not only presumptuous effrontery but quite possibly a fool's errand, an enterprise doomed to failure. This omnium-gatherum of photographs, quotations, and essays serves not as an explanation of the enigma but a suggestion of its boundaries.

Clarence John Laughlin was born near the city of Lake Charles, Louisiana, in the southwestern corner of the state on August 10, 1905. While he was still a young boy, his family moved to New Orleans, and with the exception of a brief sojourn to New York in the early 1940s and time spent in Washington, D.C., during World War II, he remained a resident of the city for virtually his entire life. His father introduced him to the world of children's literature and fantasy through the public library in New Orleans, and the young Laughlin was fascinated with books from then on. His personal library at his death numbered some thirty thousand volumes on subjects as varied as science fiction, Victorian erotica, contemporary sculpture, and illustrated fairy tales, and included runs of avant-garde periodicals. The omnivorous (though never indiscriminate) range of Laughlin's taste in books, magazines, and literature provided a self-constructed underpinning for his work in photography.

Like so many important aspects of his life, Laughlin's career as a photographer was essentially of his own making. During the depths of the Great Depression, when he was approaching the age of thirty, he taught himself the fundamentals of the medium using simple cameras and home-made enlarging equipment. In the first ten years of his career, Laughlin was employed by the U.S. Army Corps of Engineers, *Vogue,* and the Office of Strategic Services, but the two decades following World War II were strictly self-directed.

During this period, Laughlin earned a modest living as a freelance architectural photographer, receiving commissions from architects in the South and Midwest to photograph residences, power plants, hospitals, and office buildings that were the tangible manifestations and solid legacy of the postwar building boom. He supplemented this income by lecturing about his creative photographic work and theories at colleges and universities throughout the United States; he was also paid for the circulation of a series of traveling exhibitions based on thematic groupings of his work. Laughlin frequently took trips combining photographic commissions, lecture dates, and photography reflecting his personal interests. These journeys, invariably by train, could keep him away from New Orleans and his borrowed darkroom for weeks at a time. Upon his return, marathon sessions to develop and print work for clients and himself were the rule.

Laughlin pursued his own interests, writing articles illustrated with his pictures on such subjects as the sculptural and decorative ornamentation in New Orleans cemeteries, the use of wrought and cast iron in nineteenth-century buildings, and the unique and imaginative qualities of American Victorian architecture. These articles were occasionally published in periodicals devoted to creative photography or architecture. The variety of subjects is testimony to his interests and his ingenuity in promoting his brand of photography to editors and publishers. *Ghosts Along the Mississippi*, a lavish volume of Laughlin's photographs and text about Louisiana's plantation architecture first published in 1948 and continually reprinted for nearly forty years, brought in steady royalty payments that allowed the photographer creative freedom.

An operating principle in Laughlin's photography was that of association and interconnectedness, especially that linked to and through the subconscious mind. A glimpse into the Laughlin subconscious is gained from examining the nearly two dozen distinct groupings that he made for his more than seventeen thousand pictures, created for the most part between 1935 and 1965. Although organizing his photographs into groups is something that Laughlin had decided upon early in his career as a photographer, he was always tweaking the groups and their contents. The ultimate arrangement occurred in the late 1960s and early 1970s: Laughlin had virtually ceased being an active photographer, and he spent several years refining the group structure and the written captions to his work. Laughlin's descriptions of these groups, beginning with Group A, "Still Lifes," and concluding with Group W, "Fantasy in Europe," are reproduced in the appendix.

These categories provide the basis for the photograph selection and commissioned essays in this work. Some liberties were taken in the presentation of these groups. For example, the "The Magic of the Object" section also includes some pictures from "Still Lifes" and "The Mystery of Space" categories. It can be rationally argued that "Still Lifes," which in-

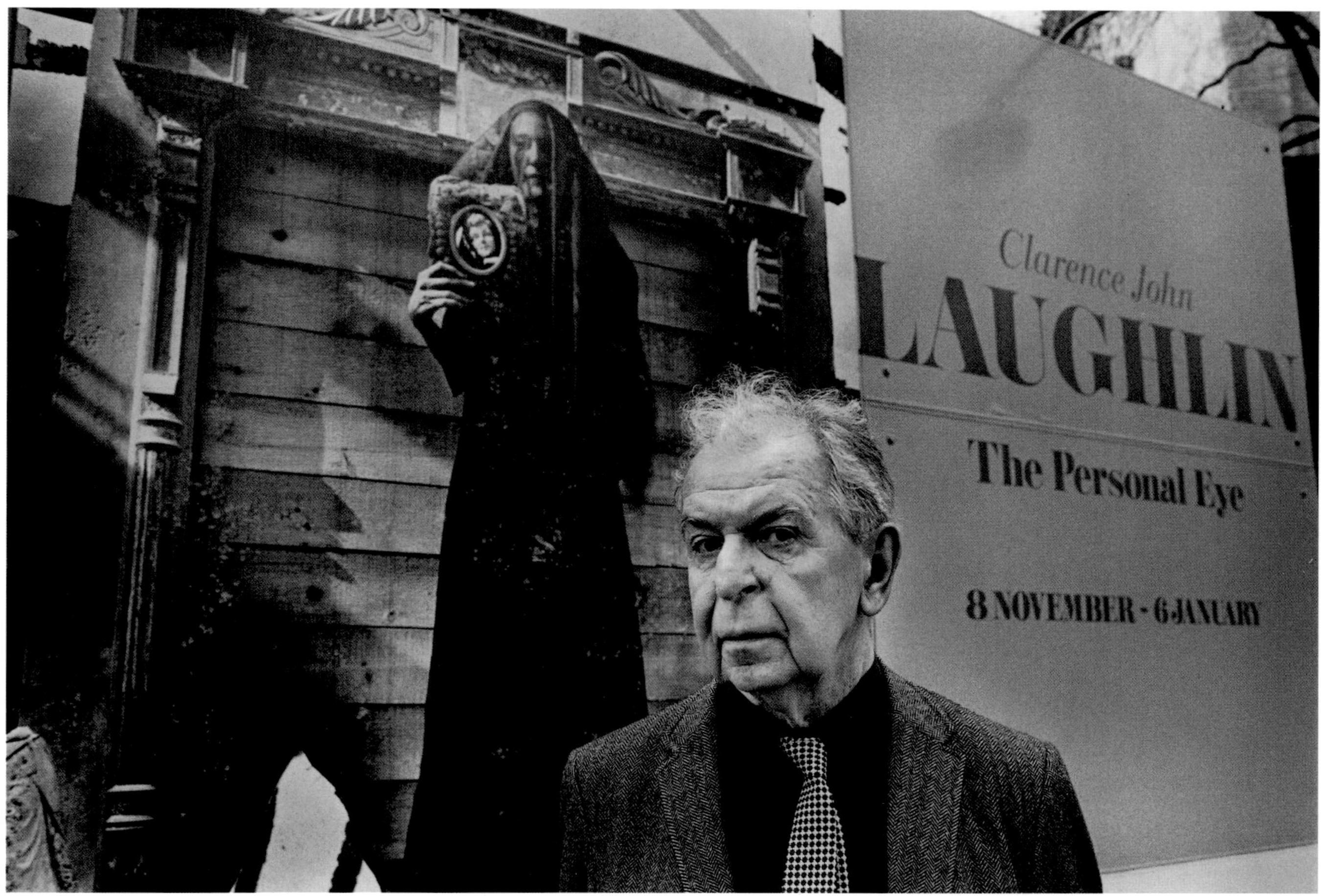

CLARENCE JOHN LAUGHLIN AT THE PHILADELPHIA MUSEUM OF ART
1973

Photoprint by Michael P. Smith © 1973; gift of Michael P. Smith

cludes Laughlin's earliest photographs, provides the formal prototypes for "The Magic of the Object" series. Many photographs in "The Mystery of Space" group were made at the same time and share similar concerns as those in "The Magic of the Object" series. Furthermore, Laughlin often assigned a particular image to more than one group and, as he expanded the after-the-fact meaning of certain images, shifted them from one group to another.

In addition to the formal intellectual structure that Laughlin imposed with the group designations, he further defined his visual intentions by the written commentary that accompanied a great many of his pictures. However compelling the photographs might be as pictorial displays, writing is what launches them into a larger realm, a world of challenging ideas. These written commentaries on specific images have often been characterized as restrictive, heavy-handed, or unnecessary. Such criticism ignores the fact that Laughlin's first and abiding interest was in the written word, even though he was recognized essentially as a visual artist; from the outset, the linkage of visual and verbal issues was paramount in his work. Laughlin argued that the specific reading of a photograph suggested by its caption was not necessarily true: although the captions explained *his* intent, they could be used as starting points for other avenues of exploration. Laughlin was a postmodern borrower decades before the term was coined: every experience, every antecedent — whether overt or subliminal — was fair game for incorporation into his work.

The after-the-photographic-fact fine-tuning that Laughlin brought to his work was part of his process. He often gave variant titles to the same work. The permutations sometimes offer a synonym for a key word in the title, and other times they entirely rethink the thrust and direction of the main idea. The care with which the titles were constructed point again to the primary role of language that Laughlin envisioned in his completed work. Indeed, he felt a photograph to be incomplete if it lacked a sufficiently poetic title and caption.

The importance of the written word to Laughlin is evident in another way. The Laughlin Archive at the Historic New Orleans Collection con-

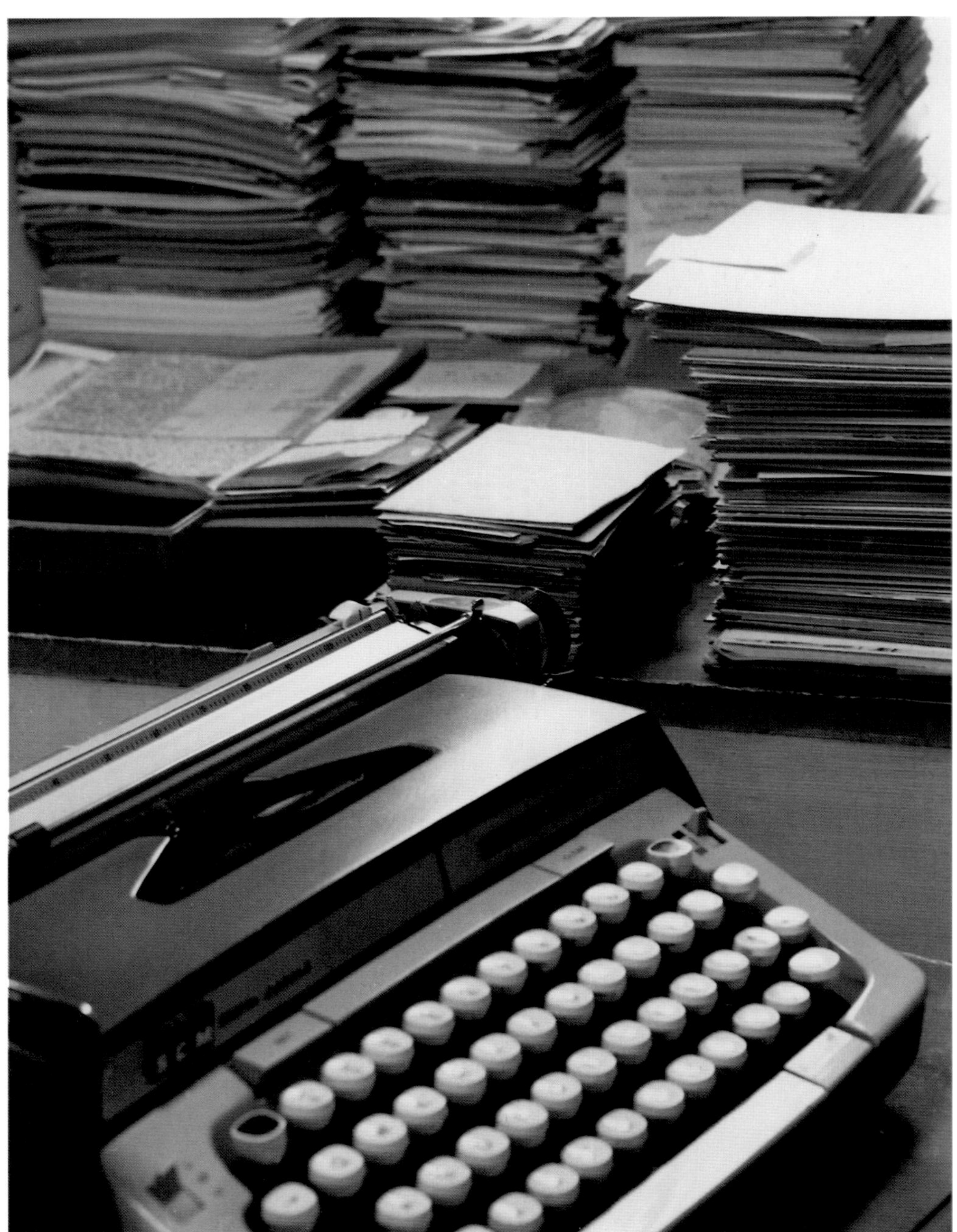

CLARENCE JOHN LAUGHLIN'S DESK
1981

Photoprint by
John H. Lawrence © 1981
Gift of John H. Lawrence

tains thousands of pages of correspondence pertaining to Laughlin's life and career. Personal and business letters, photographic logbooks, audiotapes of his lectures, and manuscripts of published and unpublished works cover the daily events and transactions, the ebb and flow of personal life, as well as providing valuable insight into his artistic process and intentions.

Laughlin was an indefatigable correspondent; literally thousands of letters were examined to extract the quotations that accompany the photographs in this book. The correspondence in the archive is two-sided: Laughlin not only preserved the letters sent to him, but retained carbon copies of virtually all outgoing letters. In letters to his friends, Laughlin, when freed from the conscious directive of creating a caption for a particular image, provides telling commentary on his own work. His written exchanges with artists, writers, and academics contain pointed and astute observations about his work. Such correspondence indicates Laughlin's sense of contemporary events in art and literature and the position that his own work occupied in that milieu. Particularly revealing are the extended exchange of letters with artist Weeks Hall during the late 1930s and early 1940s and fiery, almost embittered, correspondence with publishers Houghton Mifflin (1938–41) and Scribner's (1946–48) concerning his photographs and writing as they appeared in print. His philosophical differences with Minor White, editor of the influential journal *Aperture*, emerge in a spirited volley of letters from the late 1950s. In his correspondence, Laughlin was never daunted by his lack of formal education, spotty beyond the grade-school level.

In a comprehensive examination of the Laughlin Archive — photographs, negatives, letters, and the intellectual presence of a vast personal library — it is not surprising that the written word takes on such prominence, permeating nearly every aspect of his photographic career. Accounts of twenty-hour workdays in the darkroom and at the typewriter (Laughlin never employed secretaries or photographic assistants) certainly seem credible given the volume of photographic and written evidence. One can only marvel that he ever did it all.

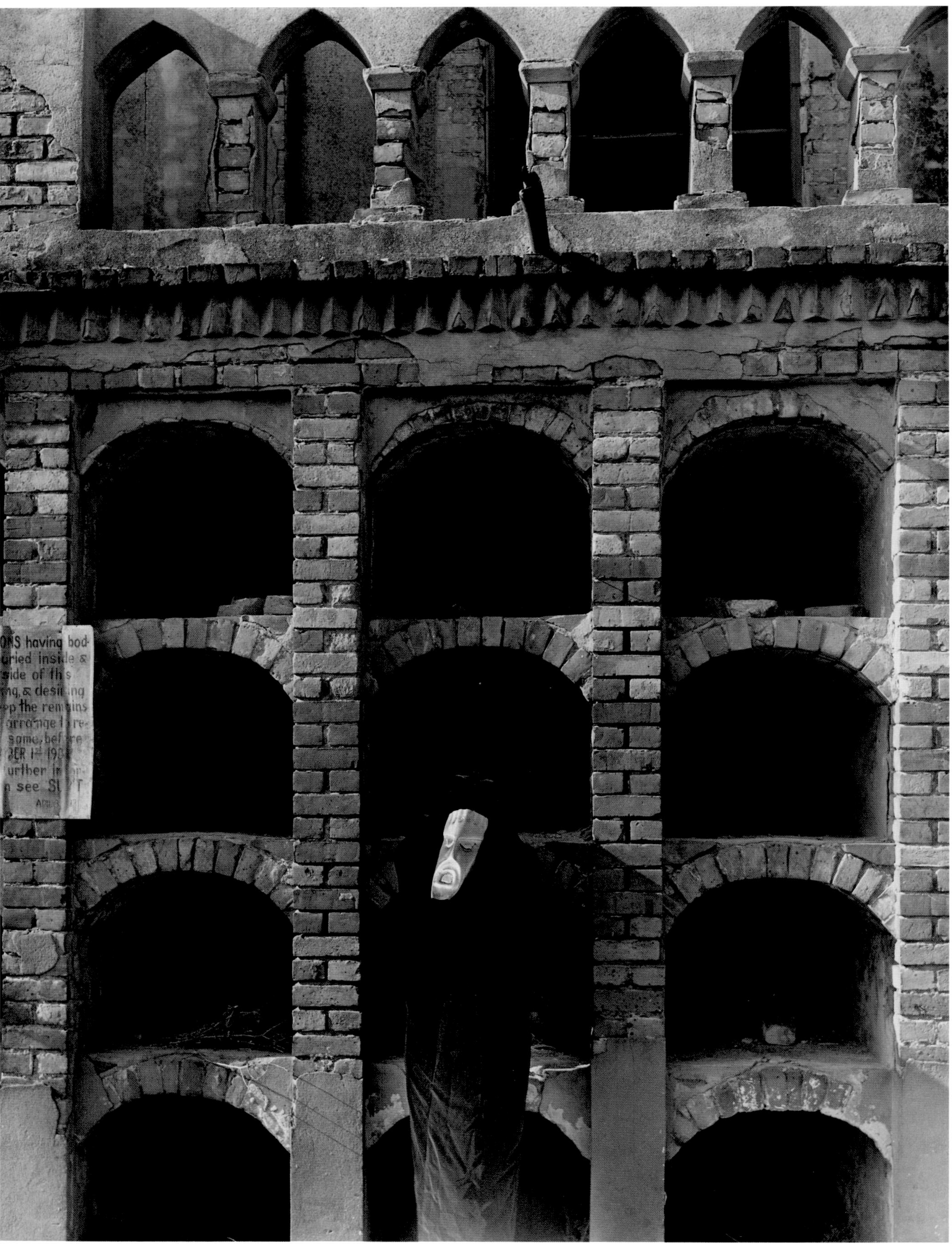
ONS having bod-
uried insi e &
side of th s
ing, & desi ing
p the rem ins
arrange
some, bef re
urther i
n see

Clarence Laughlin: The Fullness of Absence

ANDREI CODRESCU

Clarence Laughlin's work is fundamentally, situationally, and poetically paradoxical. It is everything that it is *not* about, and it is relentlessly in search of the tension between what it presents and what it intends. What it presents is a lavish fullness that intends to illustrate a variety of absence. His ruins are possessed of a complex and mysterious life. His living figures, on the other hand, are melodramatically attempting to achieve the complexity of ruins. The ravages of time are intensely erotic, while the evident eros of his humans is masked, veiled, and obscured.

Perversely, this paradox pertains also to Laughlin's aesthetic. He undoubtedly intended his photographs to be a radical inquiry into certain questions that appeared eternal but were in fact made familiar by the manner in which they were posed by midcentury existentialism. Among these were the crisis of faith brought about by the Bomb, and the implacable hostility between reality and expression. The loss of meaning and centrality for a quickly receding self, the chief themes of Sartre's *Being and Nothingness*, were adopted by artists in various ways. Many French writers committed themselves to an idealized Left that provided them with an (arbitrary) momentary faith, preferable, one assumes, to nationalism or suicide. The New York painters of the late fifties, who took Ezra Pound's modernist cry to "make it new" to heart, gave themselves over to the vital (and destructive) dictates of spontaneous form. For the American Beat writers, the revelation of the essential absurdity of modern life became an occasion for both celebration and a search for primary vitality in sex, myth, and the myth of sex. Clarence Laughlin, living in New Orleans, amid the debris of cultures that had already questioned themselves to death several times over the past three centuries, must have felt keenly the despair of the various losses documented by the existentialists. He adopted their themes, but chose surrealism — the most literary of all our century's movements — to express himself. Surrealism, which is shockingly and self-consciously "revolutionary," is also profoundly conservative: it uses all the available materials. Its chief technique is collage.

Opposite:
SAVAGERY SPEAKS FROM OUR CITIES
1941

Clarence John Laughlin to Weeks Hall, April 11, 1941

I despise "arty" technique but I dislike equally the use of the camera as a mere recording instrument. I am trying, instead, to create purely visual poetry, and to use objects as symbols of states of mind.

Laughlin was a surrealist investigator who had at his disposal the rich de facto surrealism of New Orleans. He pursued his investigation voluptuously, with an aristocratic sense of time. The luxury of his chosen medium must have made him feel guilty: most of his contemporaries were formally ascetic. To assuage this intellectual dilemma, Laughlin resorted to a diversion. He burdened his pictures with writing. His writing is diversionary; it is meant to divert attention from the pictures. This writing points (wrongly) to obvious surface paradoxes in his work, formulas that belong to surrealism and existentialism. The words mean to cover up what are the more troubling, more profound, and more seductive mysteries of Laughlin's work, the "local" ones. These belong uniquely to Laughlin and to New Orleans.

The surrealist aesthetic gave Clarence Laughlin a license to hunt mystery in his own city. But while the signature on the license may have belonged to André Breton, the sensibility that made use of it most closely resembled that of Charles Baudelaire. After Eugène Sue's *The Mysteries of Paris,* artists found that they didn't need to travel far in search of the exotic, that the places where they lived were as fully mysterious as the "fabulous Orient." The quintessential poet of Paris, Baudelaire, recast the city as a wilderness.

Babel d'escaliers et d'arcades,
C'était un palais infini,
Plein de bassins et de cascades
Tombant dans l'or mat ou bruni;

Et des cataractes pesantes,
Comme des rideaux de cristal,
Se suspendaient, éblouissantes,
A des murailles de métal.

—"Reve Parisien," 1857

A maze of stairs and arches formed
an endless palace filled
with basins where the bright cascades
fell into tarnished gold;

Like crystal curtains, cataracts
streamed down metal walls,
shimmering where the ripples made
perpetual descent.

— Translated by Richard Howard
(in *Les Fleurs du Mal,* Boston: David R. Godine, 1982)

Opposite:
THE CLAW FROM THE DRAWING ROOM
1939

Clarence John Laughlin's caption

This was the very first picture made for the series which was first called: "Poems from the Burning Cities of our Time," then, later, called: "Poems of Desolation" and finally called "Poems of the Interior World." There is an inner sequence to the pictures in this series, but none of the pictures was made in the final sequence.

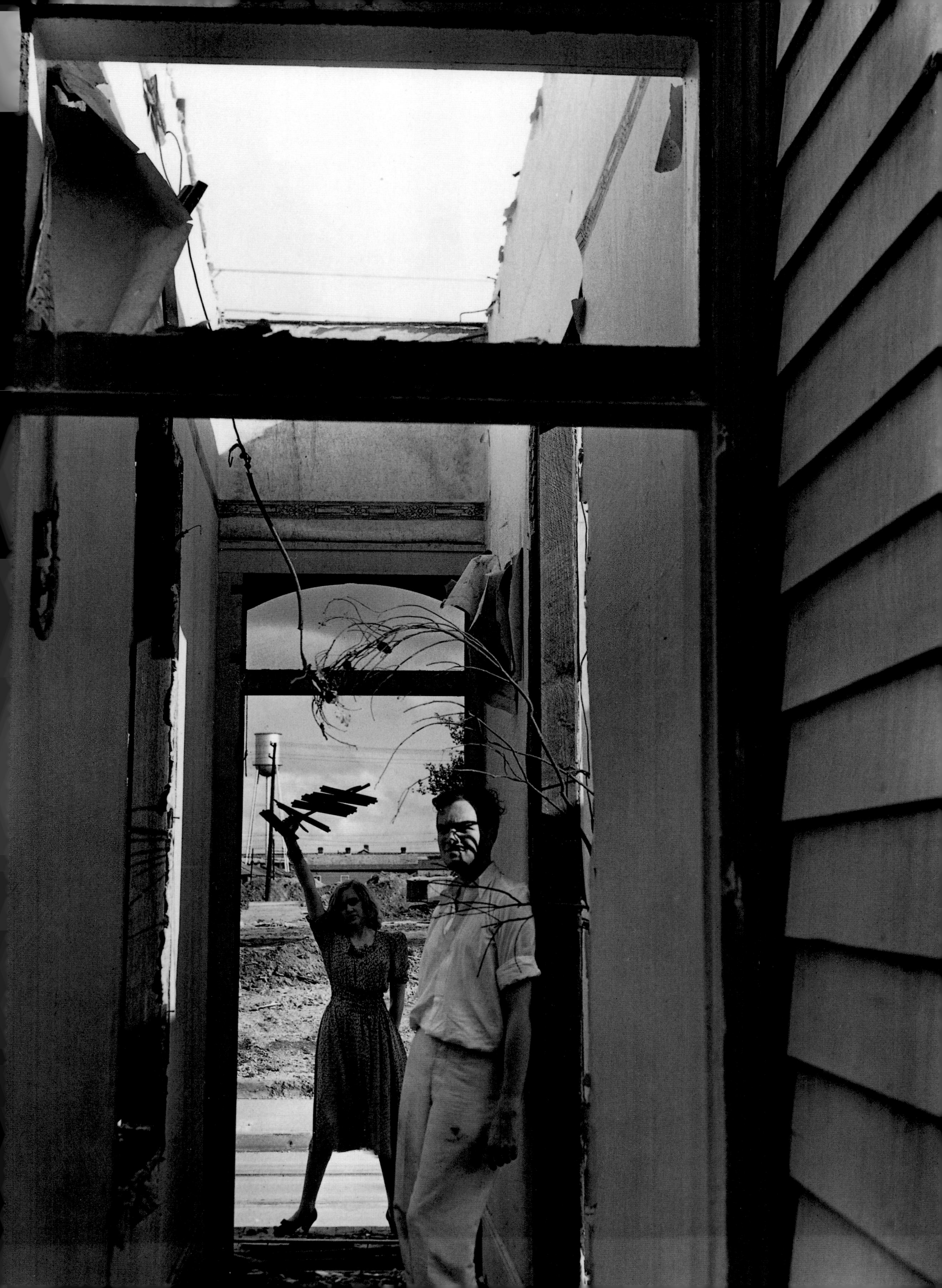

Clarence Laughlin is the Charles Baudelaire of New Orleans. The particular feeling Baudelaire called "spleen," which is a mixture of melancholy, rage, eros, and resignation, radiates from these photographs. The "black sun" of Baudelaire and of the surrealists illumines Laughlin's New Orleans with its funereal rays.

And yet, these are not depictions of an "interior world" as the writing saboteur in Laughlin would have it. They are dramatic descriptions of an intensely evocative city that revels in its masks, shadows, plays, and confusions between past and present. New Orleans confounds the outsider in everything, beginning with its geography. A city *under* the river? The question of "self" under these circumstances is better confined to the frame. The "outside" has more "self" than the "inside."

The photograph entitled "We Try to See through the Mirror of Self" is a perfect mirror of this artist's sensibility, including its anguished theoretical frame. But it is an infinitely more mysterious image than its resolute and assertive surrealist frame. The poetic title to the photograph, as well as the text that accompanies it, pays homage to the Sigmund Freud of the surrealists. (To be distinguished from the Freud of Lacan or of the neo-Marxists, for instance.) Laughlin's text takes care to let us know that "[s]elf is like a mirror which, when viewing the world, reflects only ourselves. Here is the symbol of those people of good will who try to transcend their selves."

Yet, in looking at the picture, one finds little of those ideas. The mourner standing before the wall of numbered graves in the New Orleans cemetery is a hole, a cutout of darkness in the paradoxically solid mausoleum. Everything about the graves in the background suggests presence: the square of each grave, the unsettling familiarity of numbers in each square. The numbered squares look like a school problem, or a television game show. Standing on top of the graves is a middle-aged, one-winged angel-rhetorician declaiming from the top something that one has surely heard before. It is Saint Bartholomew with his arm in a cloak. If he is indeed holding forth on the mirror of self, he looks like an unlikely spokesman for it. He stands atop too much poetry. The "grave" irony here is lush, like medieval memento mori inscribed on a copulating couple. This is, of course, surrealist *humour noir*, but it has a peculiarly local flavor as well to anyone familiar with the numerous graveside rituals of the populace. But if the tomb is all presence, the mourning figure before it is not. The living being before the grave is more absent than the dead before whom she stands. In Laughlin's photographs of New Orleans the dead are always more alive than the living. This too is one of the fundamental qualities of this city. The dead are not hidden in New Orleans: they rise from the ground like the dead of William Blake who "aspire to that golden clime/ where my sunflower wishes to go."

I once took a Polish friend of mine, a poet, to the Lafayette Cemetery

Opposite:
WE TRY TO SEE THROUGH THE MIRROR OF SELF
1941

Robin Feild to Clarence John Laughlin, September 6, 1945

But I do hope that they [photographs for a Newcomb College exhibition] will include a whole lot of what I call your metaphysical prints. As you know, I feel very strongly that your work along these lines is pushing the periphera [sic] of visual symbolism to the limits.

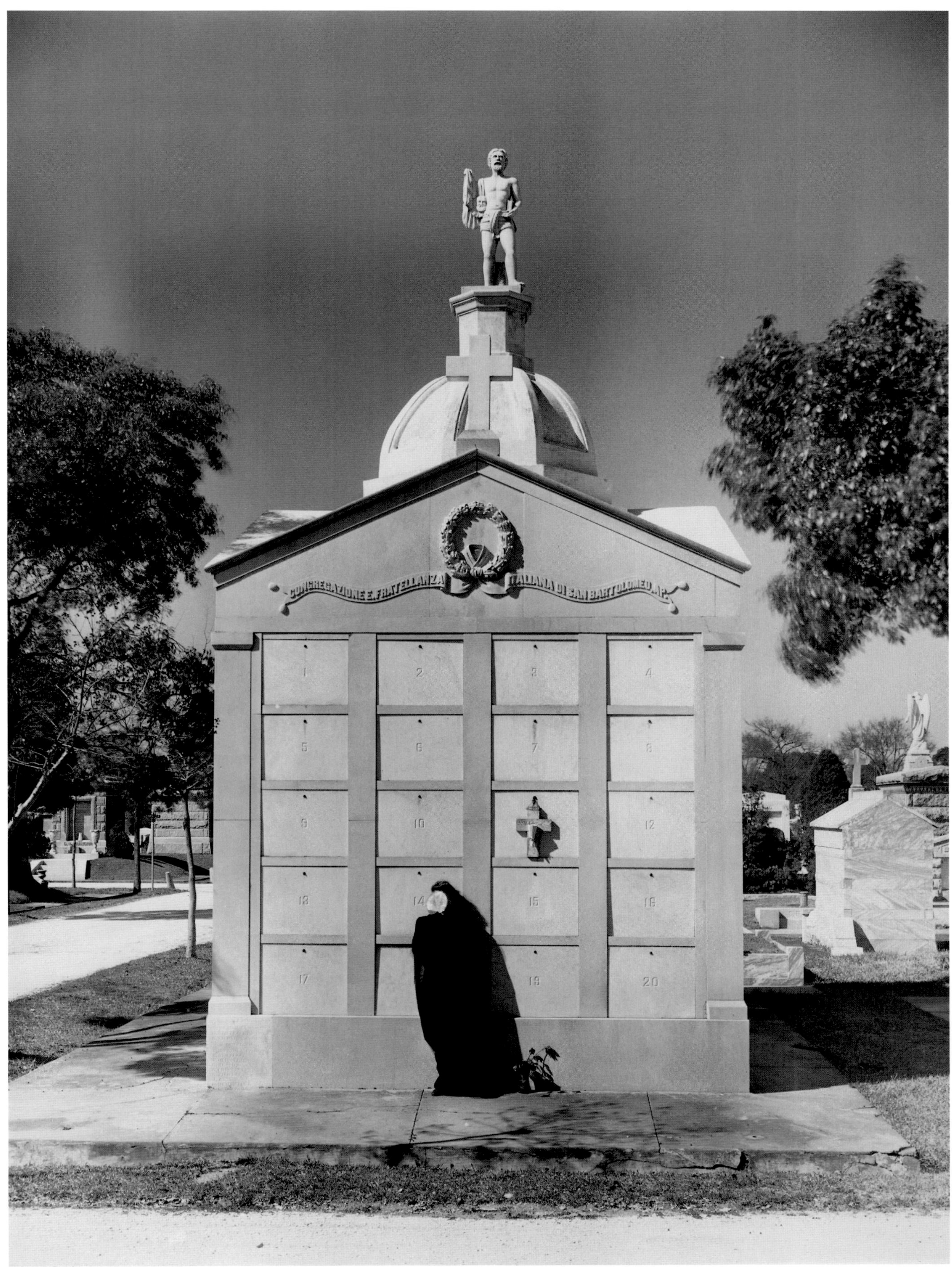
CONGREGAZIONE E. FRATELLANZA
ITALIANA DI SAN BARTOLOMEO A.P.

to have coffee. We sat on a grave and I told him that this was my coffeehouse, where I came to write. He told me that he had once organized a student strike in Warsaw and had taken his classmates to the cemetery, where they studied the graves for "the true history of Poland, not the history they taught us in school." The graves of Warsaw became, for that brief time in the age of lies, the living truth.

Laughlin's graves are not documentary in that sense. They are not even particularly political to the extent that his writing wanted them to be. What they teach, if anything, is the frisson of twilight, the voluptuousness of pleasure among those hopelessly immune to it. Laughlin's graves encourage lassitude and decadence because they let us feel the intellectual artificiality of the anguish that possesses his models. The radical rhetoric of titles like "Love Has Become Death," "Our Hearts Were False," "We Have Sowed the Seeds of Ruin," would not have been out of place among the graves of Warsaw. At the same time, it is only in New Orleans that their paradoxical strength is activated. Such dramatic clarity needs the impressionistic sabotage of humidity and the sensuality of decay.

The Romanian poet Lucian Blaga said, "Our duty when confronted with a mystery is not to explain it, but to make it more mysterious." The mystery of Clarence Laughlin's photographs continues despite his efforts to explain them. Looking at his masked, posed models, his well-tempered mixtures of flesh and stone, his studies of mortuary forms, I am seized by a kind of giddiness, a fin de siècle impatience. I want to seize the heart of evening in the city of the dead, an oddly erotic proposition.

Opposite:
THE BLACK GATES OF OBLIVION
1940

"The Camera as a Third Eye" (1945), published in The Professional Photographer *(September, 1951), 24–29, 50*

I am not concerned, then, with photography in a narrow sense — its fascination for me is related to my interests in modern painting, in social questions, and in the nature of light and of time. The mystery of light, the enigma of time — form the twin pivots around which all my work revolves.

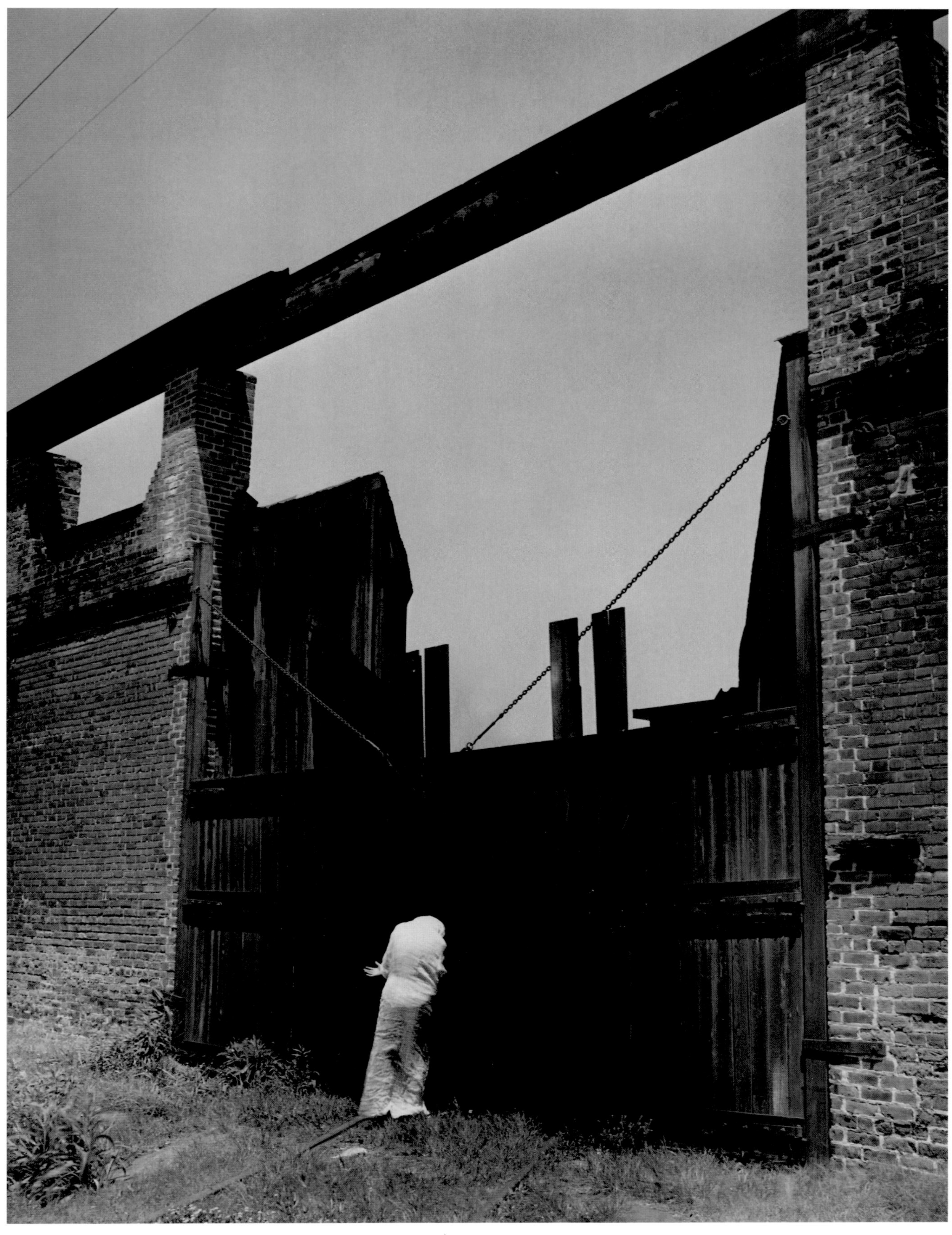

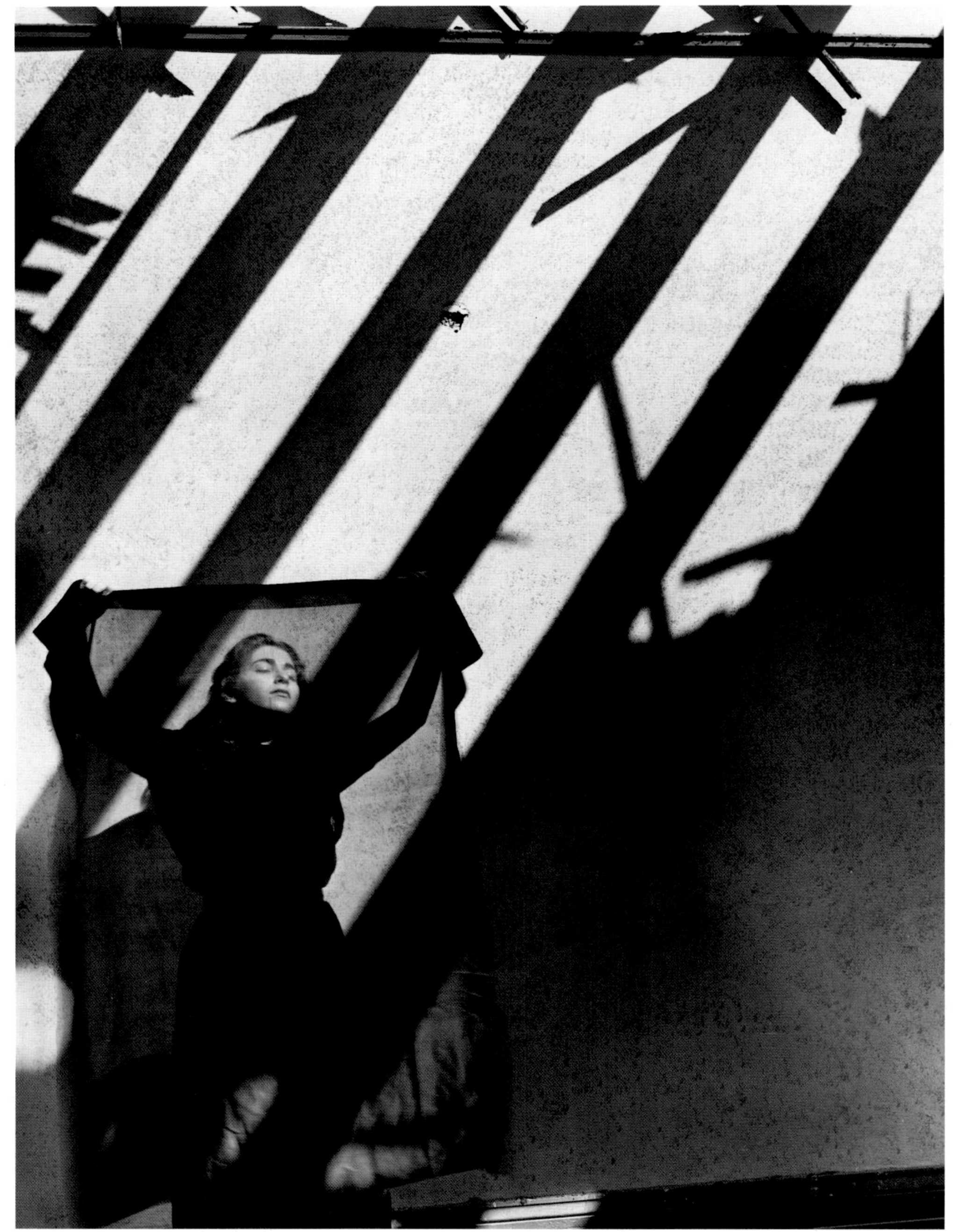

DEFINITE AND INDEFINITE

1940

Clarence John Laughlin to Bryan Holme, March 10, 1946

Unfortunately, ["Poems of the Interior World"] is far beyond the imaginations of the commercial publishers of the United States, I am afraid.

Opposite:

THE HOUSE OF HYSTERIA

1941

Cedric Wright to Clarence John Laughlin, May 17, 1950

I have seldom met anyone who has the kind of knowing which you do.

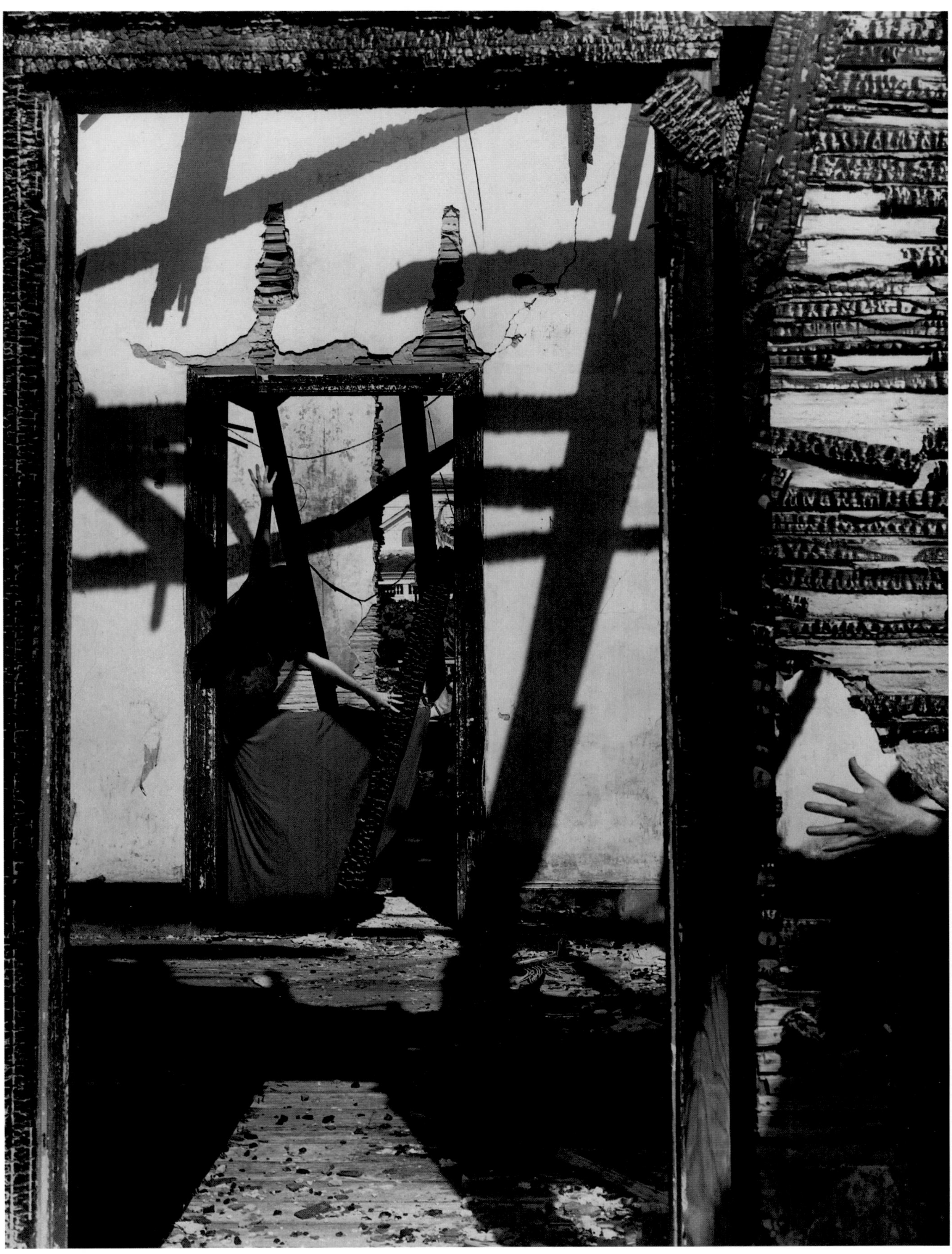

Opposite:
DWELLER IN AN EMPTY HOUSE
1940

Clarence John Laughlin's caption

One of the symbolic photos dealing with the aftermath of the appearance of the dictators. Civilization became an empty house from whose window looked forth and the phantasm of all that was dead and vacant. And the shell, which, normally, is a symbol of resurrection, becomes part of a figure of death.

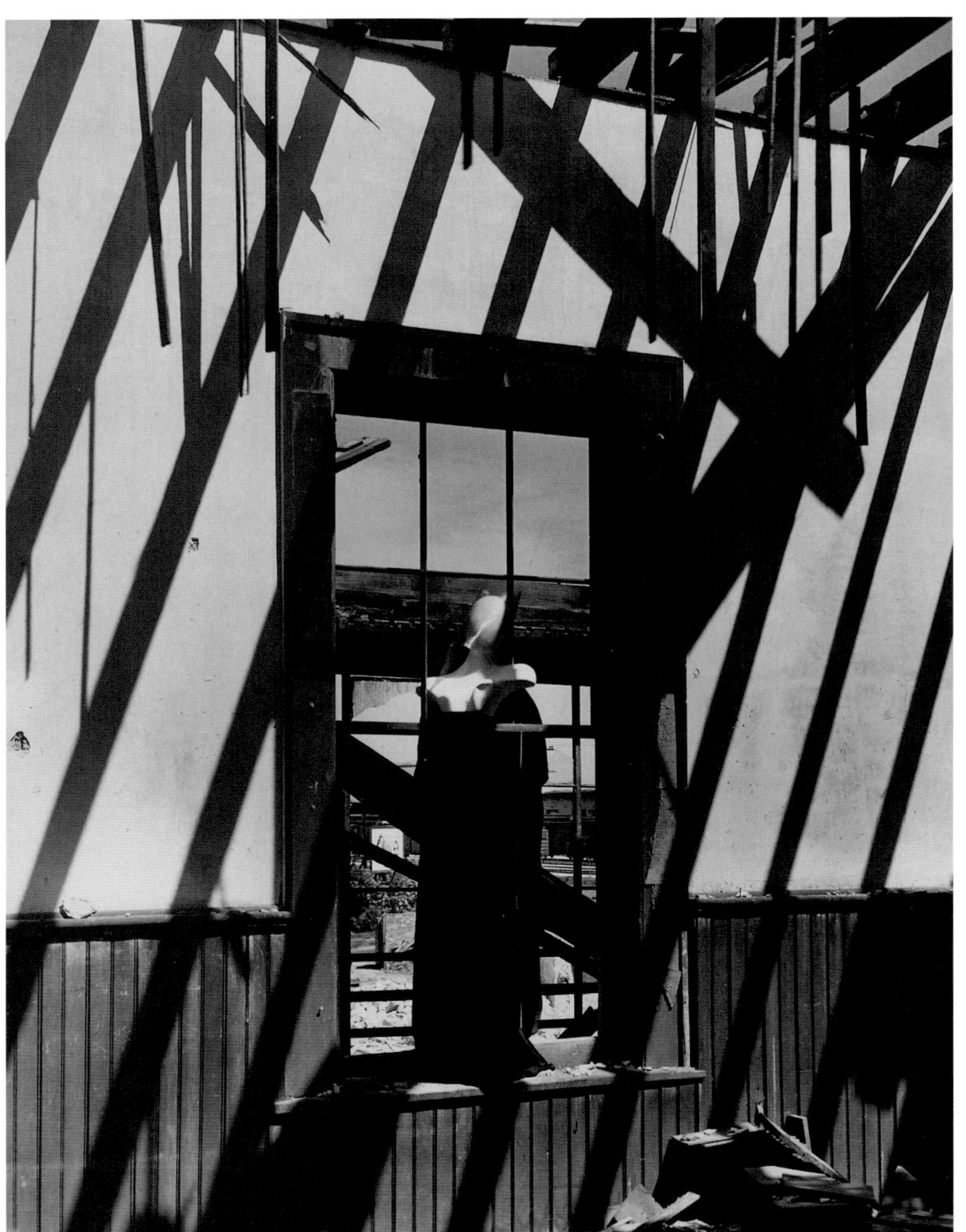

OUR PRISON BARS ARE SHADOWS, NUMBER ONE
1949

Clarence John Laughlin's caption, as printed in Gallery Series Two (Chicago, 1968), 37

But anonymous man still has his fears — many of them induced. . . . Just as the shadows, here, become more solid than the walls — so, too, do his intangible fears become more solid than steel — confining him in a kind of cage wherever he goes.

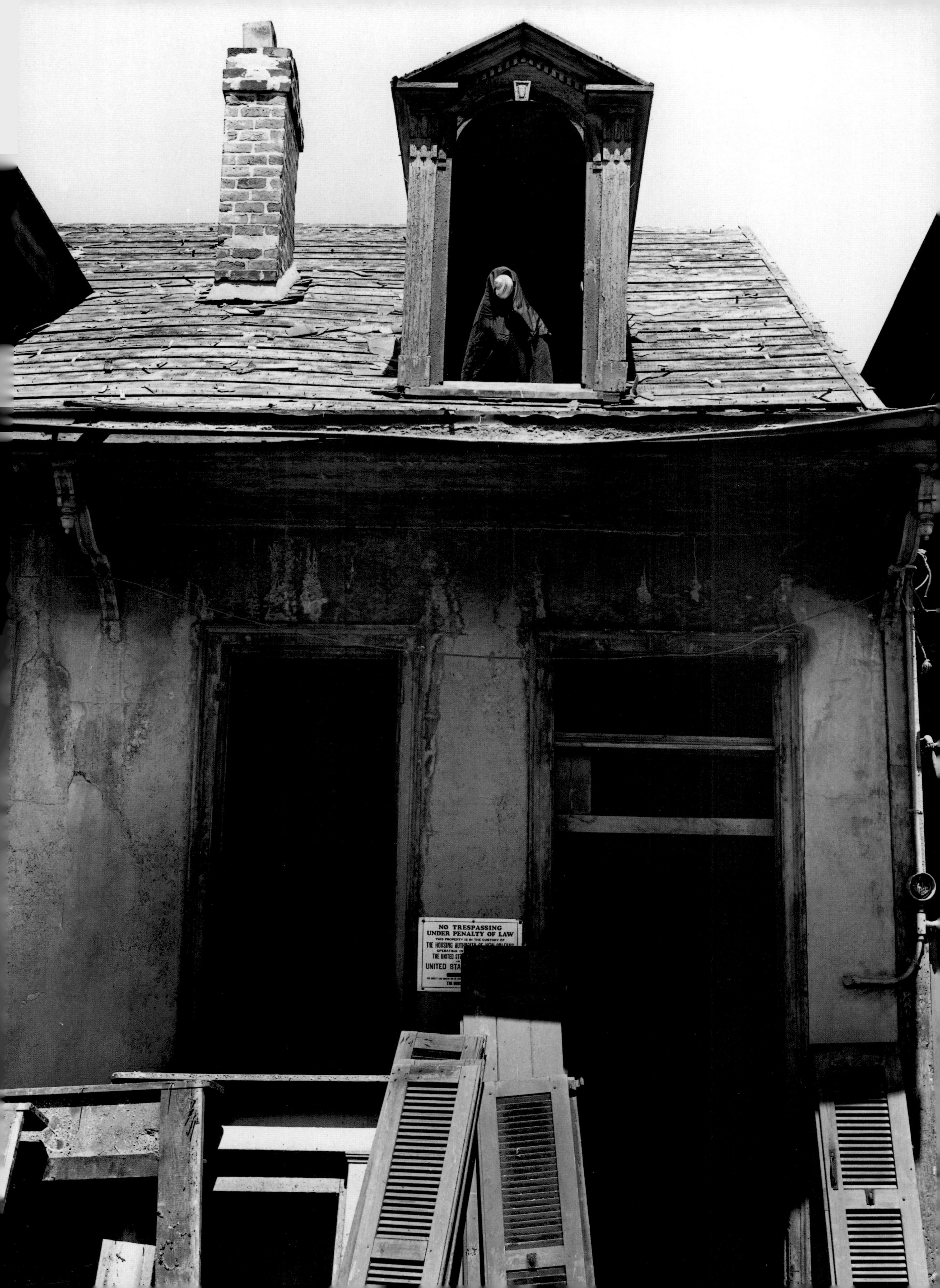
NO TRESPASSING
UNDER PENALTY OF LAW
THIS PROPERTY IS IN THE CUSTODY OF

Opposite:

EMANATION OF RUIN, NUMBER FOUR

1940

Clarence John Laughlin's caption, as sent to Eugene Berman, July 13, 1941

This print belongs to a series entitled Poems of Desolation, a series in which the photographer is attempting to avoid the merely "recording" function of the camera, to create, instead, purely visual poetry: to use objects so that they will become symbols that externalize completely the fears and desires of contemporary men — their confusion, and the crumbling world in which they live. In this particular print the photographer has used a shattered wooden frame structure, reminiscent both of the 1890s and the war-torn cities of the contemporary world. Each of the window and door openings has a different visual effect. The two figures on the top floor do not seem "posed" — they have become, instead, concretions of fear, fear that renders the black and white emptiness of the room more sinister, and the frivolousness of the woodwork more inane.

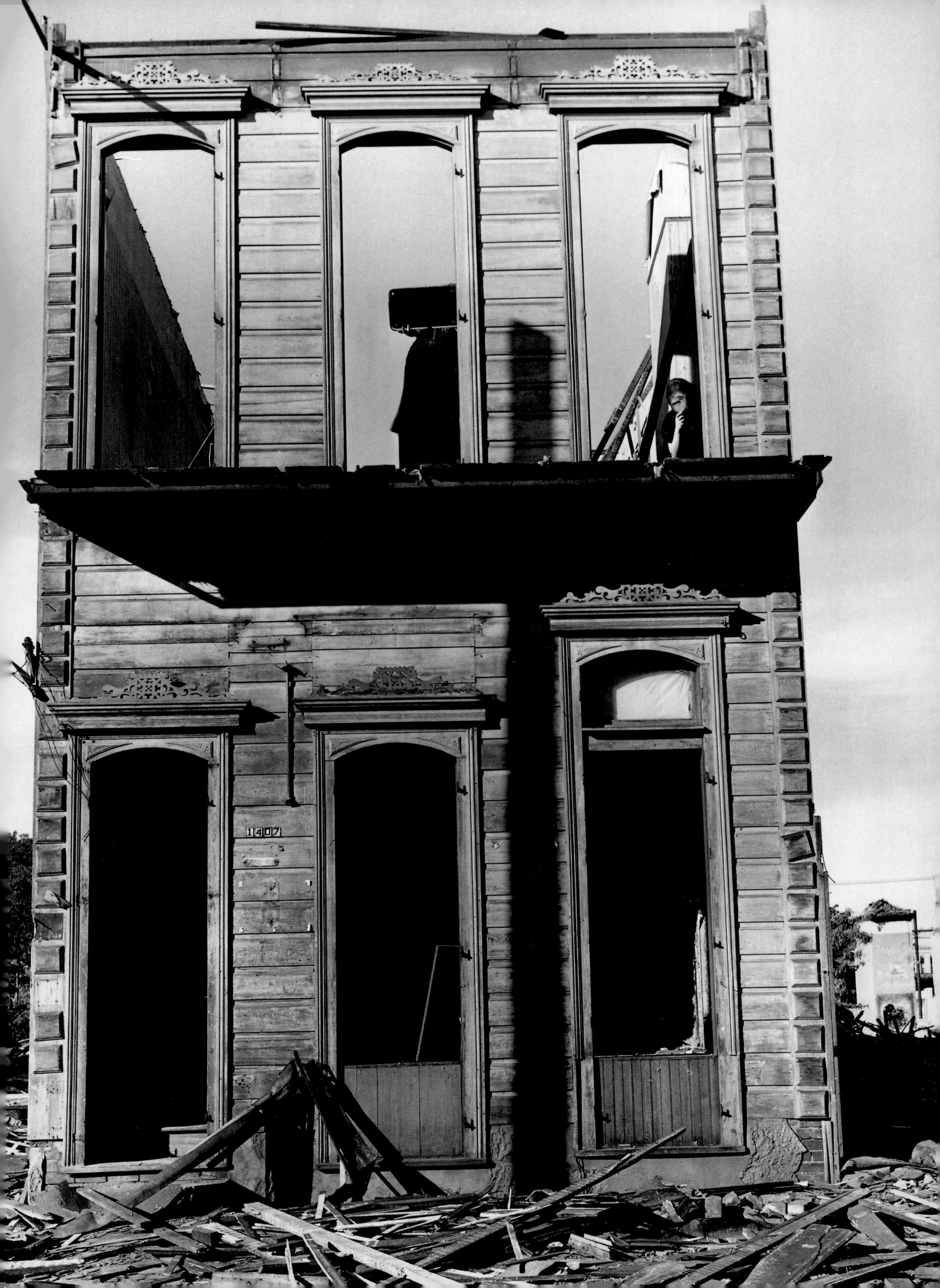
1407

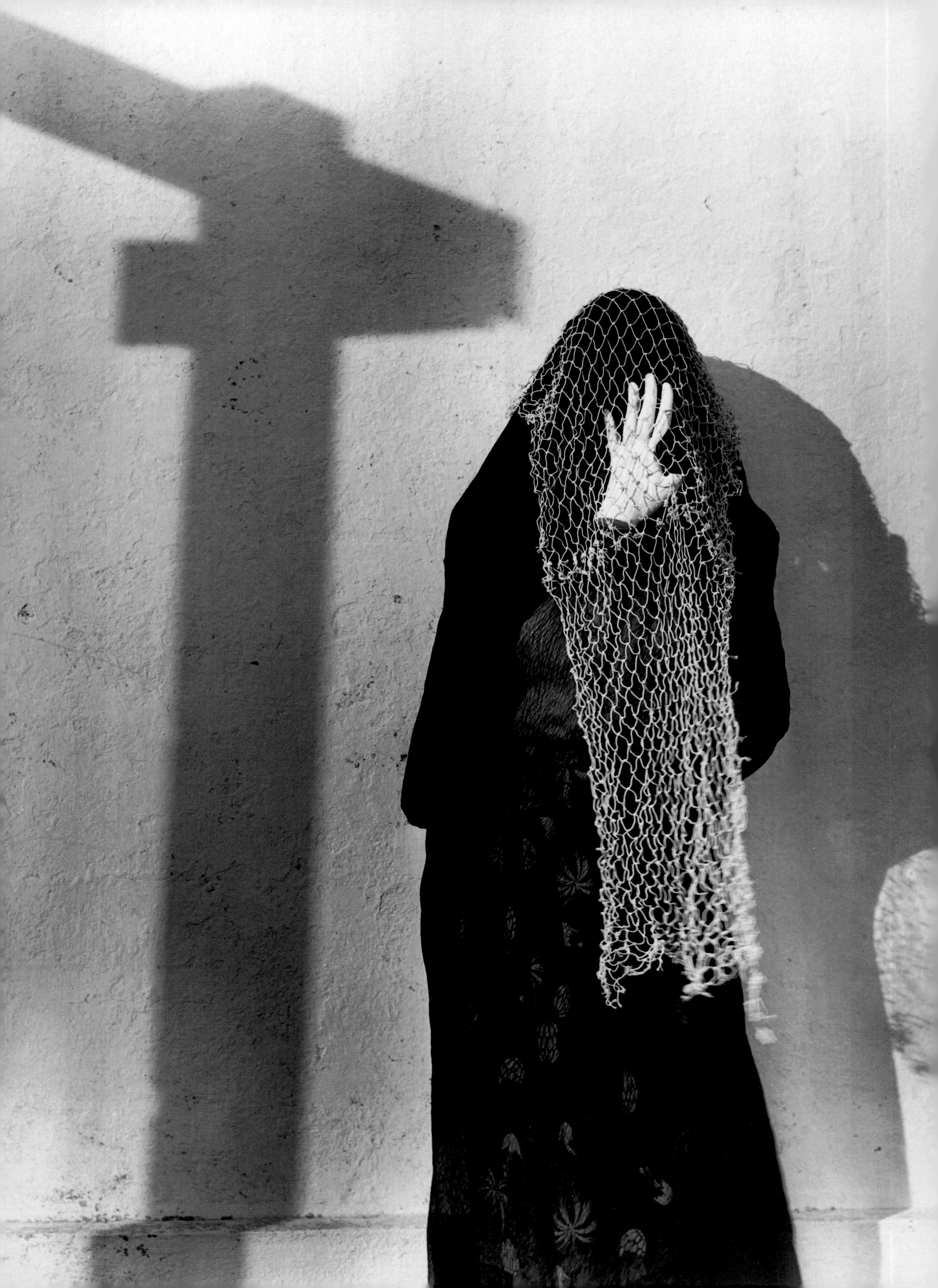

Opposite:
SIGN POST TO NOTHINGNESS, NUMBER TWO
1941

Clarence John Laughlin to Paul Brooks, September 23, 1941

It is not that my pictures need explanations as pictures; it is rather that the material I am using in my pictures needs a much more complete discussion.

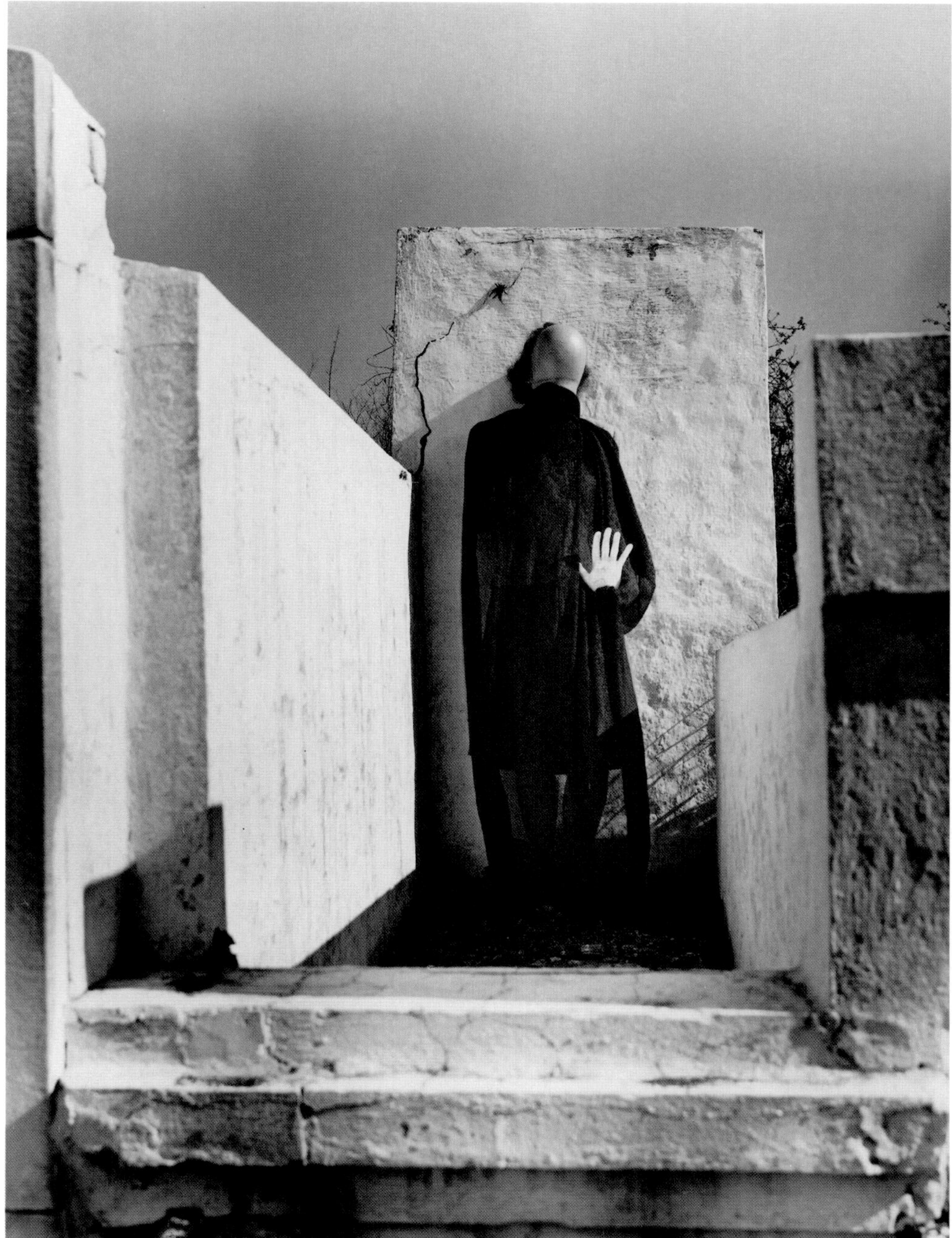

THE WHITE HAND OF DECEPTION, NUMBER ONE
1941

Clarence John Laughlin's caption

Satirical symbol of the politicians and the seekers for power who, while they carefully conceal their true natures, and purposes, extend the white hand of deception.

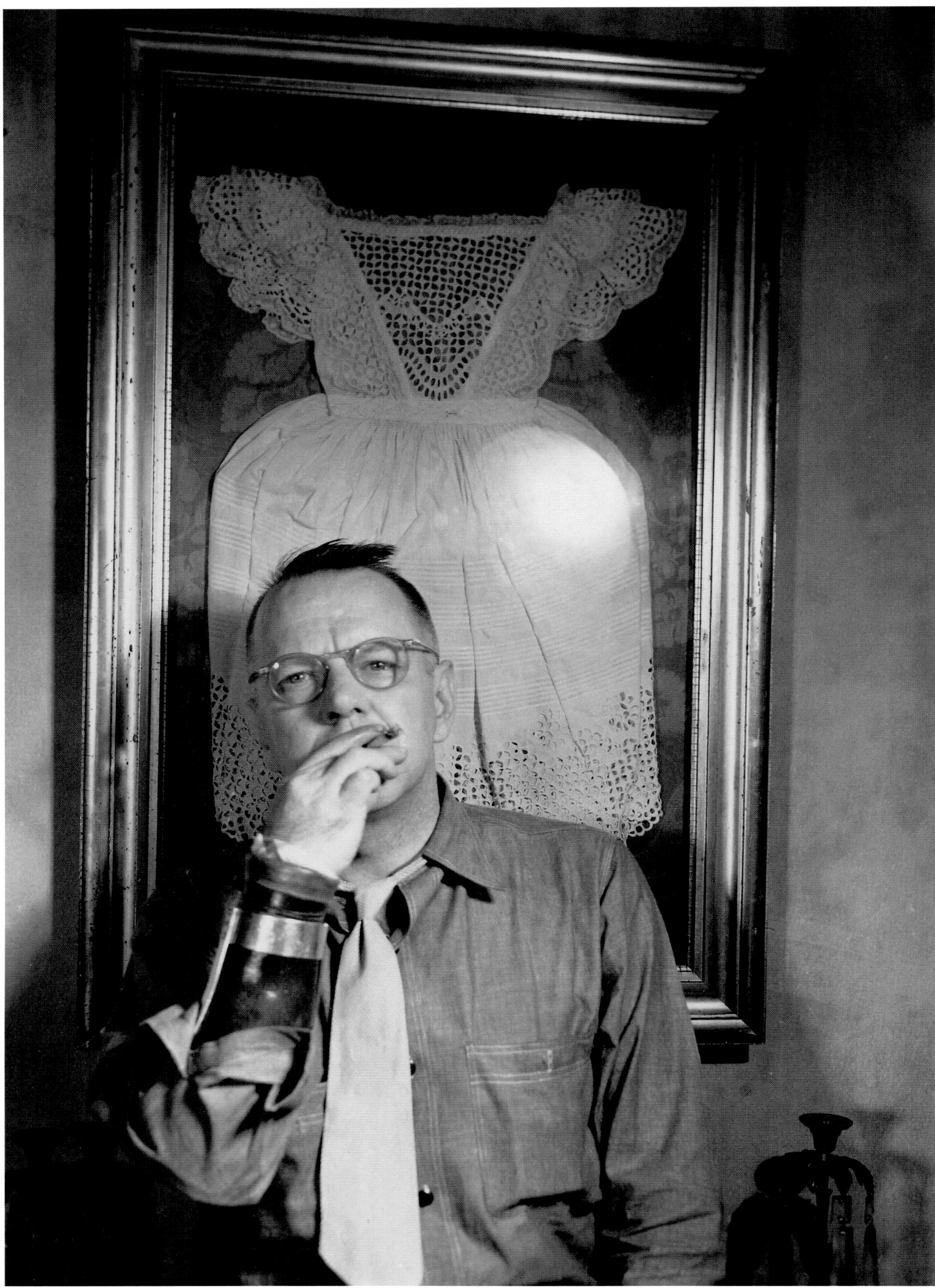

VISUAL POEMS

Clarence, A Celebration

ELLEN GILCHRIST

Everything about Clarence was mysterious, magical, surreal. So it came as no surprise to me when the package of photographs for this section of the book arrived in the mail and turned out to include a photograph Clarence gave me years ago to use as the cover for my first book. It wasn't the one he would have chosen, but he let me have my pick. He was a generous man, never more so than when he was overriding his desire to control everything in sight in favor of being his loveliest and most polite.

The book was a collection of poems and contained a poem about an adventure Clarence and I had with a group of surrealists from Chicago who had come down to pay him homage.

Clarence was mad for poetry, especially the French symbolists and surrealists. He would stop whatever he was doing to entertain poets or talk to them long into the night about art and beauty and imagination and the workings of the unconscious mind and how it made such fabulously obvious statements when a good receiver was holding the pen or the camera or the brush.

Visual poems, he called them, these photographs that told a thousand poems a thousand ways without needing a word of explanation. Still, Clarence insisted on explaining, until at last, near the end of his life, he began to type up explanations of the meanings of the photographs and would go around to galleries and affix them to the inside of the mounting of the frames. I remember the first time I saw one of these altered frames. Joshua Paillet was standing before it in his gallery sighing and smiling the smile genius calls up.

This is what genius is, isn't it? Genius means a new thing, a thing no one else is doing or has done or can or will do. Genius says, here is my mark. I am the genie of this place.

Alone in the darkroom, shall we say, with the image coming to life in the developer, Clarence's imagination would begin to run rampant through all the possible meanings of a moment in human time. His friend, Weeks Hall, standing against a wall holding a cigarette. Behind him is a framed

Opposite:
POSSESSED BY THE PAST
1939

Weeks Hall to Clarence John Laughlin, 1939

I hadn't had my picture took [sic], with the exception of a passport, since my days at school. It does have an unusual air and what I call a timeless one, which all good works of art should possess. Even all good period things are timeless, if you know what I mean.

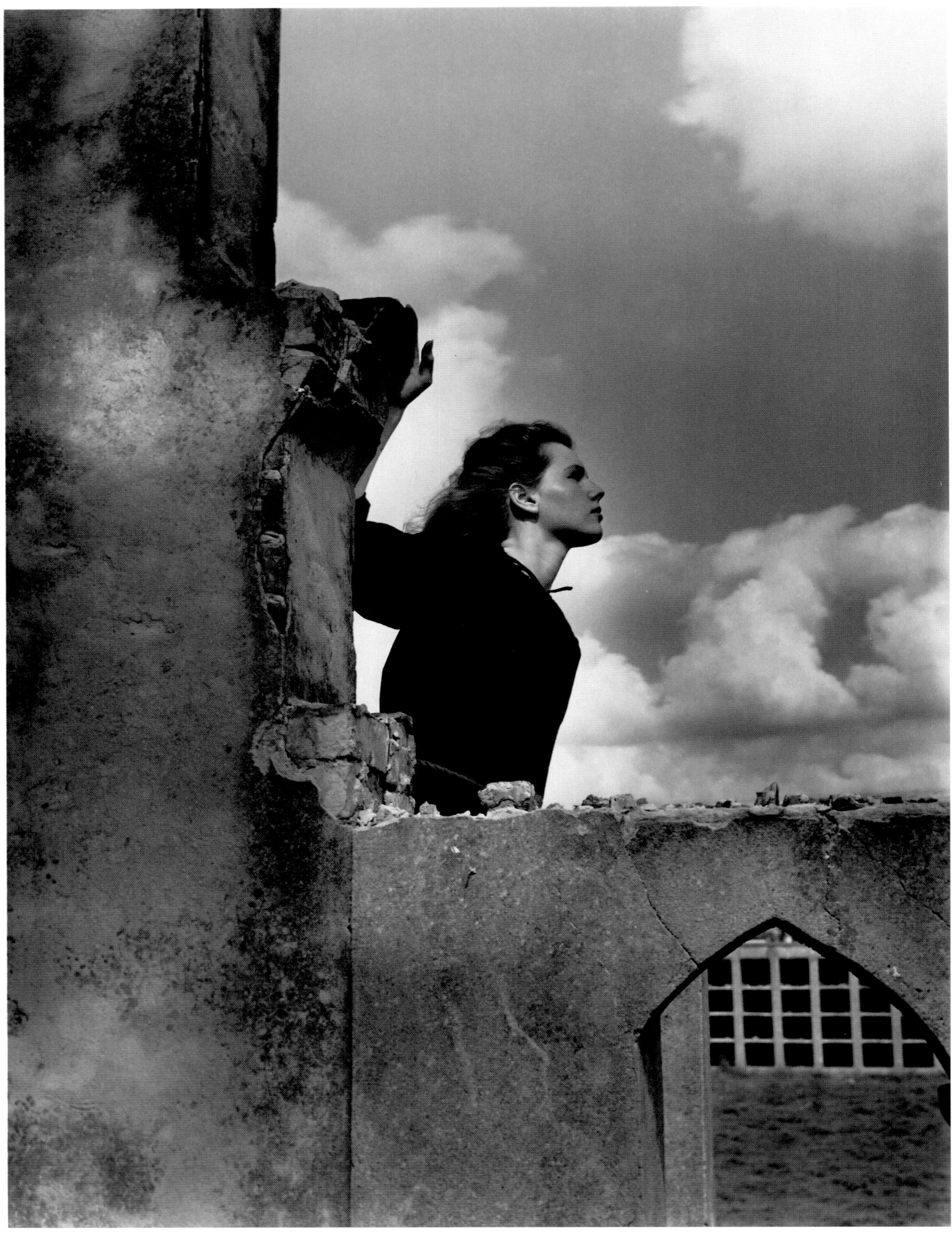

white organdy pinafore, trimmed in lace. What could Clarence not read into this? Life, death, love, self-destructiveness, rising and falling, good and evil, the Oedipus complex, rivers, skies, gods and goddesses, and the source of all water. And so, not wanting the viewer to be stuck with the impoverished leavings of a normal imagination, Clarence would begin to write the pages that were to accompany these already perfect and boundless metaphors.

. . . Of course, in order to sell his work, Clarence had been forced many times to listen to stupid questions about his art or to well-meaning praise that seemed to him reductive or untrue. His vision was so sure and so intense that he felt a mission to transcribe the entire experience for the viewer or the listener. Many times he told me stories of how he had gone to some place to take a photograph carrying pounds of equipment and come home carrying pounds of books. He did this until he wore out the cartilage in his knees. He brought the books home for many reasons. Because he collected them. Because many of them were rare and in danger "of being cut up and sold by greedy dealers," because he wanted to be surrounded by myriad examples of other men's and women's art, because he believed all art was one great creation and that art was man's truest heritage and duty and trust.

The photograph he gave me for my book is called "Figure Head." Of the model he would only say, "She was a Welsh actress. She married a wealthy man and disappeared into the Garden District." There she stands, in the moment Clarence snapped the shutter, forever young and vibrant and beautiful, with the wind in her hair and her lovely profile daring the sea. The sea? Or the future? Or the thought of herself being photographed by a genius? How many epics have I written about this woman as I passed the photograph on my wall or picked up somewhere a copy of my book.

The photograph Clarence called "Woman Contemplating a Statue" seems to be the same lovely Welsh face. This photograph contains all the surreal dissociative elements Clarence prized in art. It is not only a stone figure the woman contemplates, but a crypt. Shadows and light. Even in the daylight Clarence wanted to remind us of death. Only in the light of that knowledge does life achieve its keenest value.

Teaching us the value of every moment is the gift of art. How beautiful we are, art says, how mysterious, how divine. Clarence Laughlin gave his life to that teaching. The gifts he left us are many, but for me, who was once a poet, these visual poems, with or without their wordy explanations, are especially dear. I was only feeling my way into my own work when I knew and learned from Clarence, when he would sit me down and get out the photographs and make me listen. Things are not as simple as they seem, he seemed to say. Things have many meanings. There are rooms within

Opposite:
FIGURE HEAD
1941

Ellen Gilchrist to Clarence John Laughlin, February 25, 1978

It will be several months before the book goes to print. . . . I believe that a book of poems is a damn serious thing. Every detail must be perfect to match the perfection of your photograph on the cover. See, you give us something to live up to.

rooms within rooms. The conscious mind is the size of a screw on the doorbell of the door leading to the house of the unconscious.

Of course, this was all very seductive to a child of the bourgeoisie. Clarence was in permanent exile from the bourgeoisie, and he taught me it was safe to find my own exile. I was once like the woman in the photograph called "In Vertical Light, Number Two." Like many of Clarence's subjects, she seems unaware of the fragility of her position. She seems to think it is perfectly nice to be perched so precariously on a wooden porch in an uncertain world with the shadows of giant plants all around her. Perhaps her biggest worry is that her lipstick isn't straight or her hose have a run in them or her stomach is sticking out.

Doors within doors within doors. The incredible richness of human memory and imagination. Like a kaleidoscope the human brain can take a few bits and pieces of light and darkness and turn them into a milliard images. Clarence believed he had found formulas for unleashing or awakening these possibilities for his viewers, but in the end he had to resort to words. Also, I no longer believe it was craft or work or dedication that produced the mystery of his photographs. I believe it was genius. No matter where he had been born and raised, he would have found a way to look deep into the layers of reality. Luckily for Louisiana, it was here that he came to be and here that he came to wonder and create.

Opposite:
IN VERTICAL LIGHT, NUMBER TWO
1940

Ellen Gilchrist, "Clarence, A Celebration"

Like many of Clarence's subjects, she seems unaware of the fragility of her position. She seems to think it is perfectly nice to be perched so precariously on a wooden porch in an uncertain world, with the shadows of giant plants all around her.

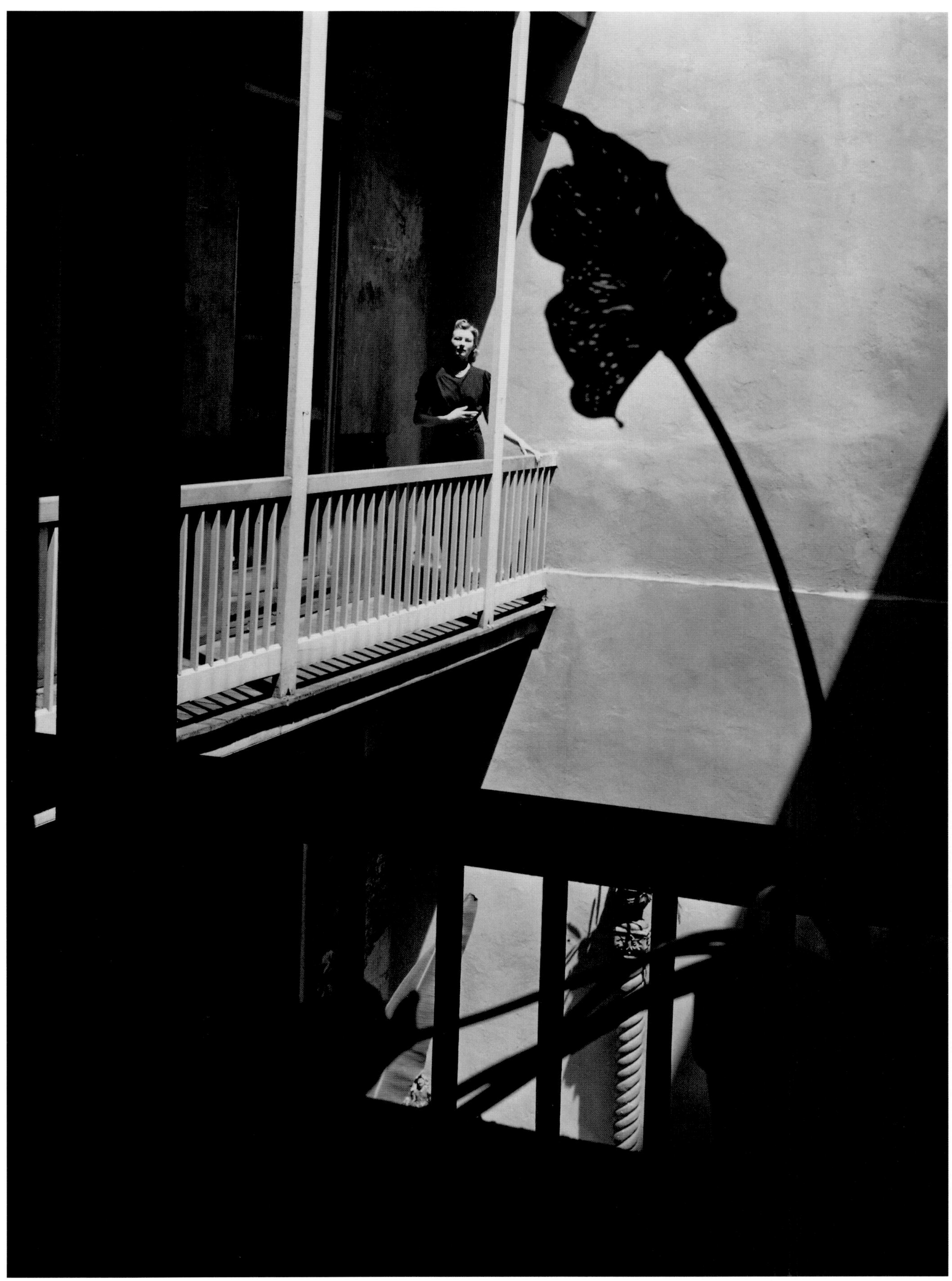

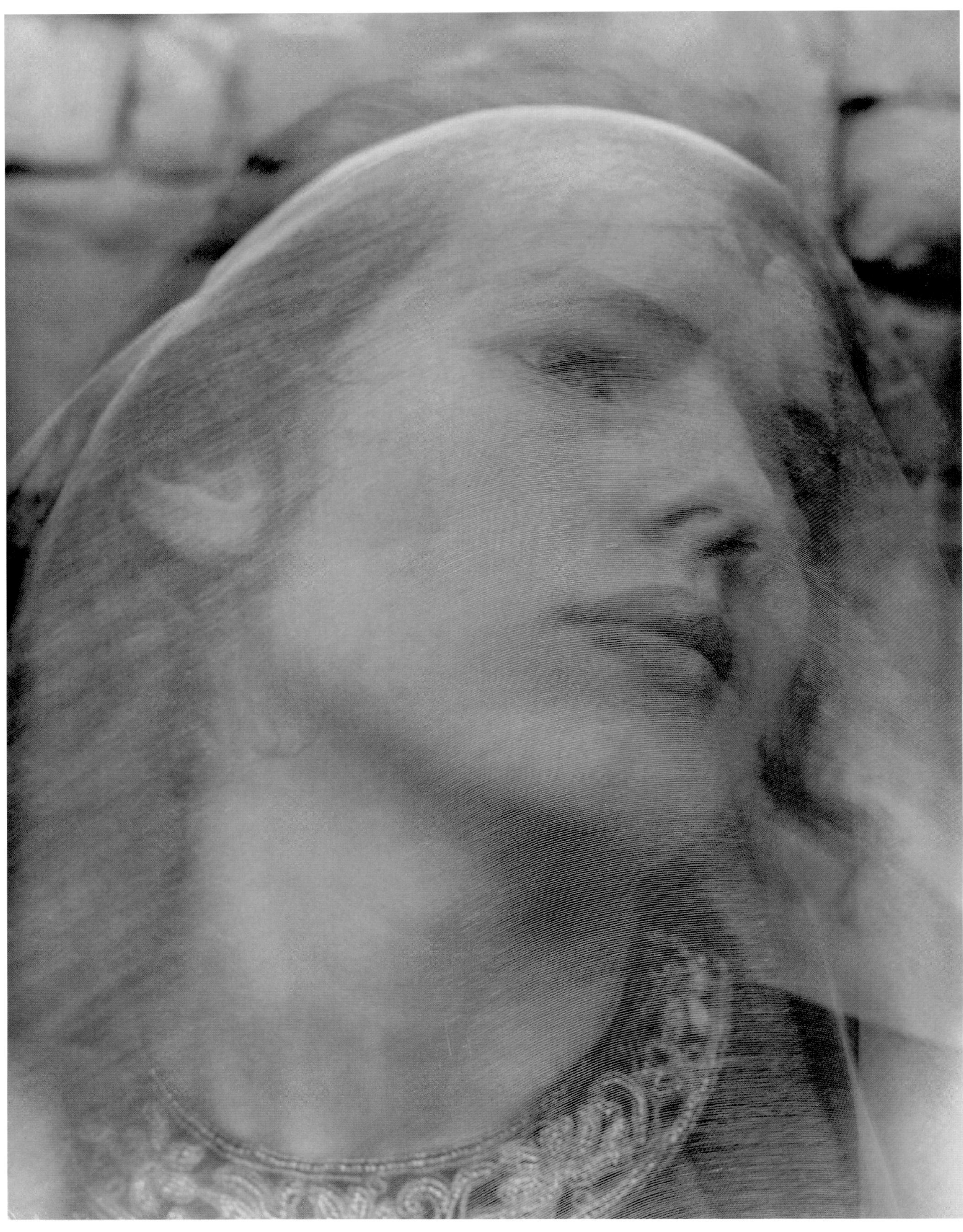

Opposite:
NOSTALGIC HEAD, NUMBER TWO
1941

"Architecture and the Camera" (August 1949), typescript

I learned that the camera is a machine only when used mechanically, that it could be made to respond to the special vision of a particular imagination.

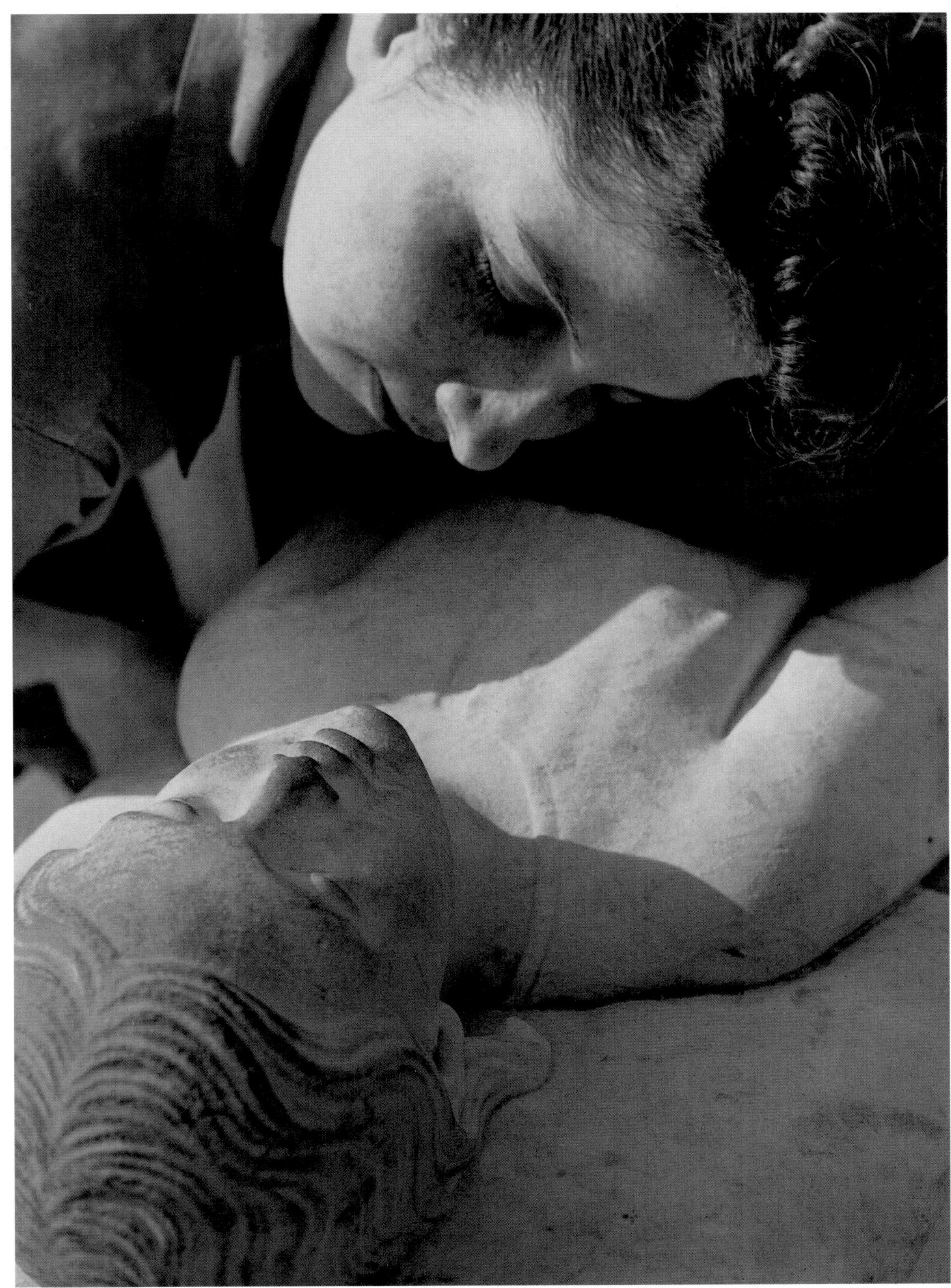

WOMAN CONTEMPLATING A STATUE
1939

Clarence John Laughlin to Daniel Masclet, October 19, 1953

It, therefore, should be possible for even the photographer — just as for the creative poet or painter — to use the object as a stepping stone to a realm of meaning completely beyond itself.

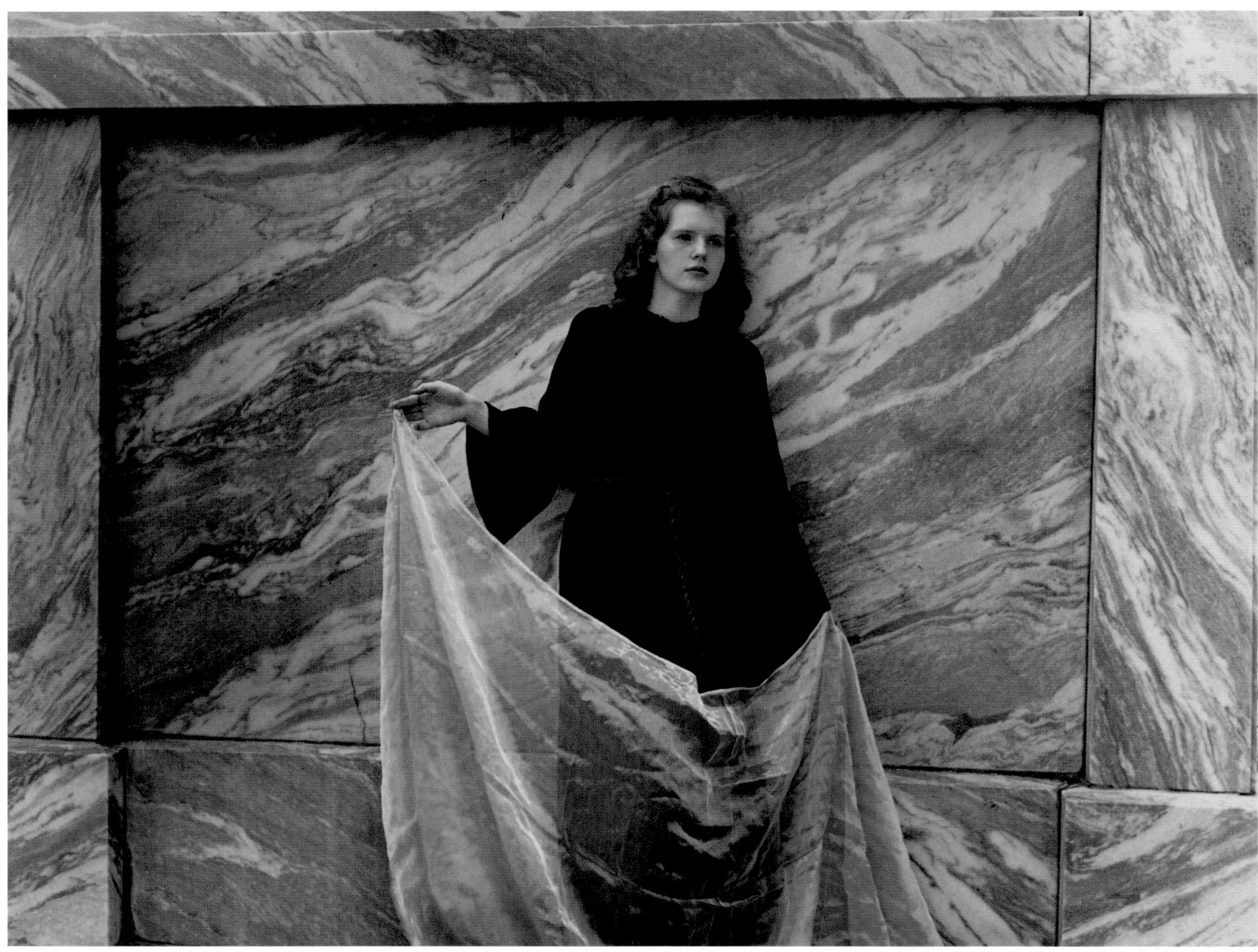

COUNTER MOVEMENT, NUMBER TWO
1941

Weeks Hall to Clarence John Laughlin, November 11, 1941

Much remains to be done with women in photography; for one thing, make them look female.

Opposite:
VISION IN A BRICK WALL, NUMBER ONE
1941

Clarence John Laughlin to Daniel Masclet, October 19, 1953

Fundamentally, in photography, I work from the inside out — rather than from the outside in — as do most photographers. This means that I only photograph things that really, really excite my imagination — things to which my mind has already been "pre-sensitized," so that I can perceive other meanings in the object — things which become catalysts, or focal points, or projections, of my own inner world.

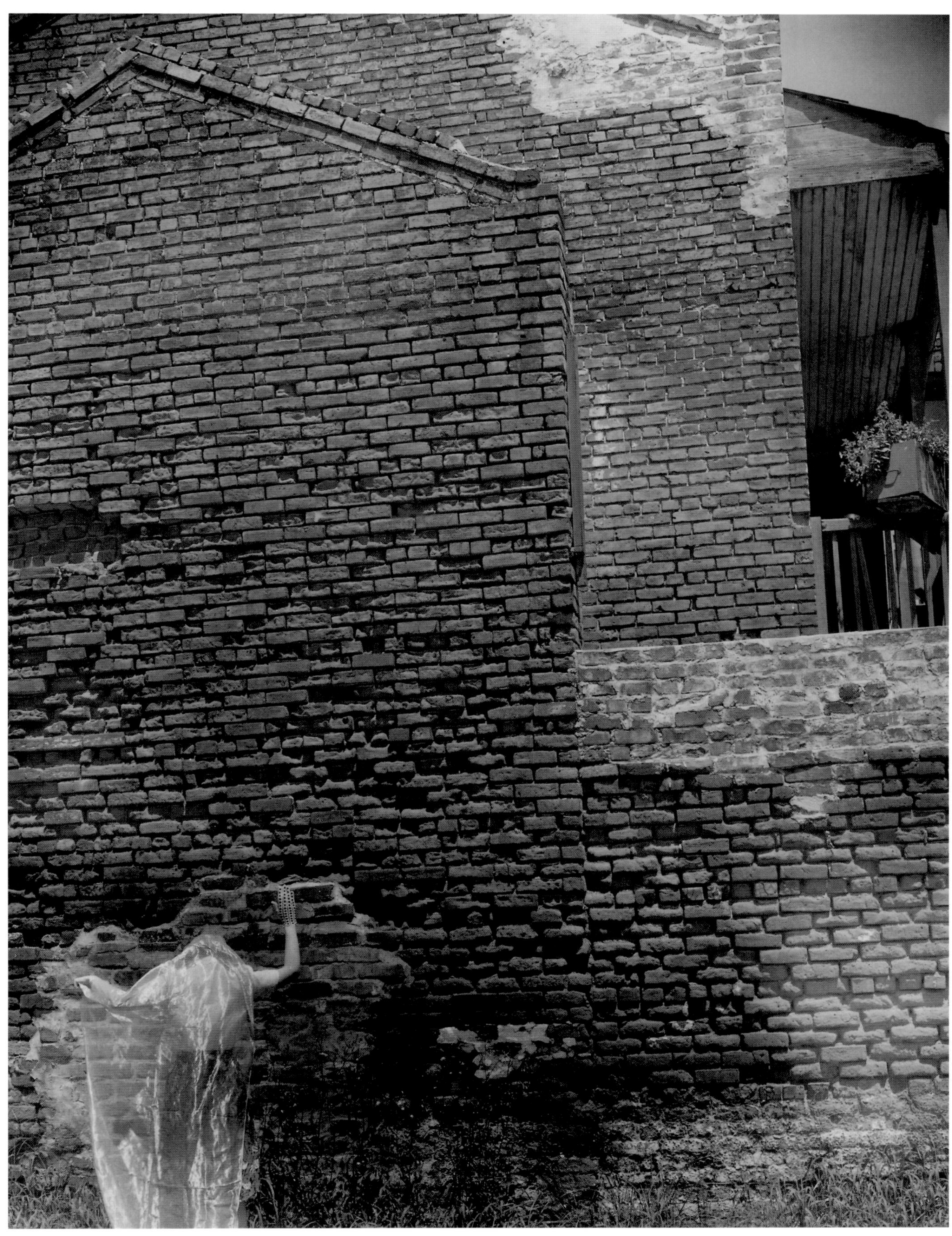

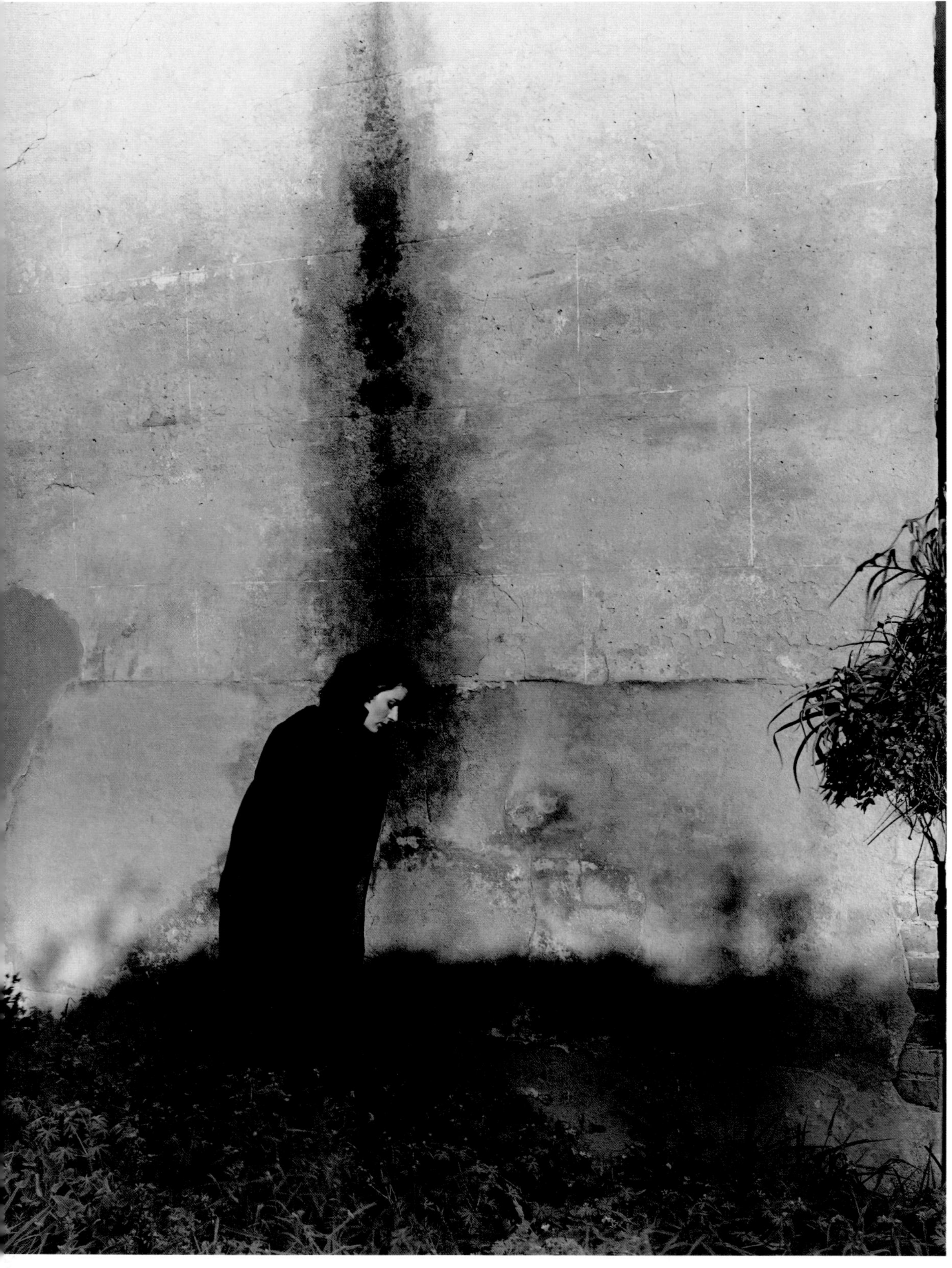

Opposite:
SHROUDED FIGURE
1940

"The Evolution of a Photographer" (1945), typescript

There have been only two chief and consistent concerns in my work: 1) luminosity — the magic of light itself; 2) the use of the object as a symbol, and hence, of the camera as a living instrument to probe the intangible psychological jungle in which every object is enmeshed.

THE RISING TIDE OF DARKNESS
1941

Wade Donahoe to Clarence John Laughlin, December 30, 1949

I look forward to further acquaintance with your work in both satire and natural fantasy. I was quickened to several passages of poetry from having looked at your photographs. Your eye sees more than any literary eye can, and what it sees is of literary significance, at least to me as a poet.

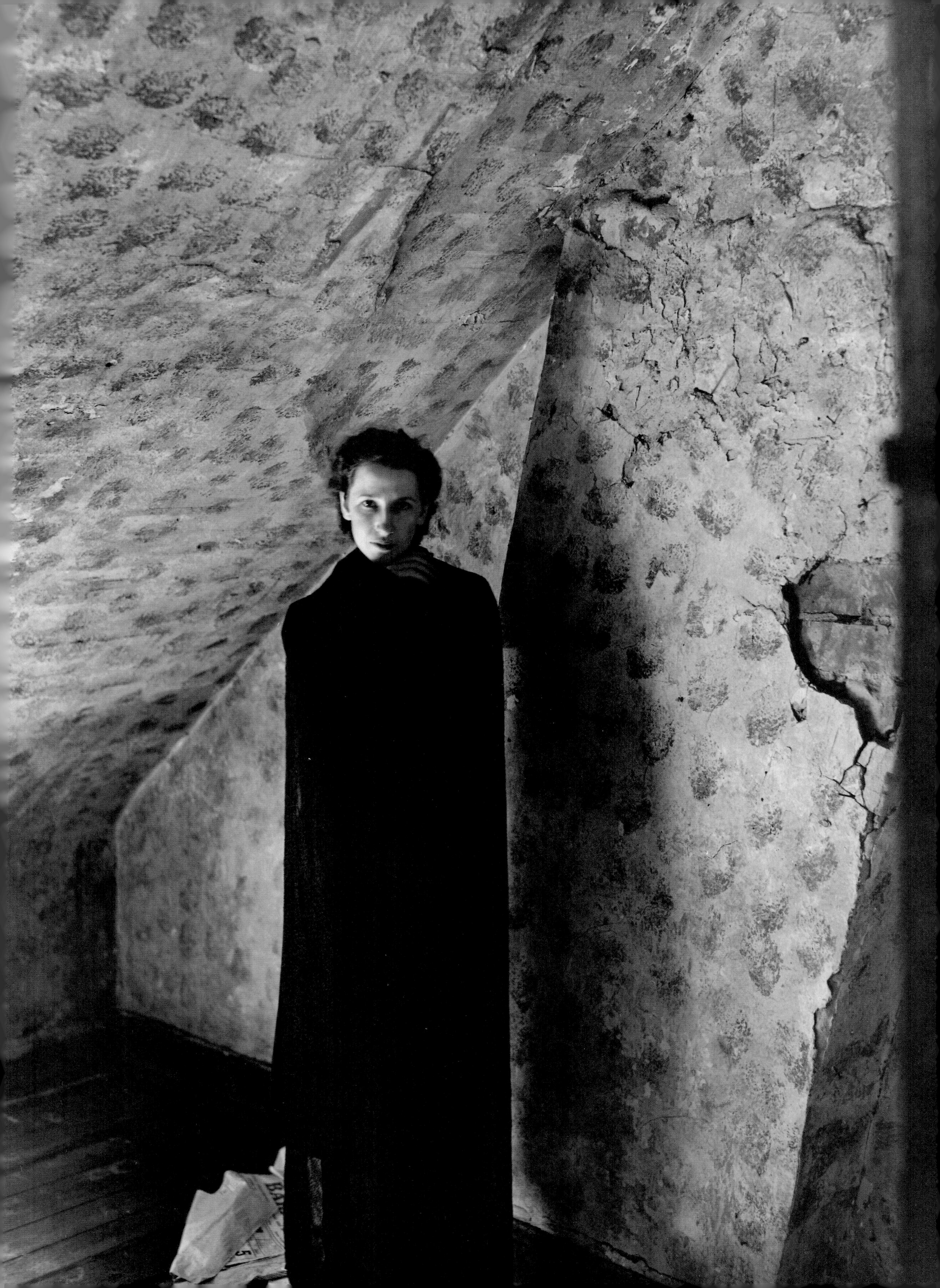

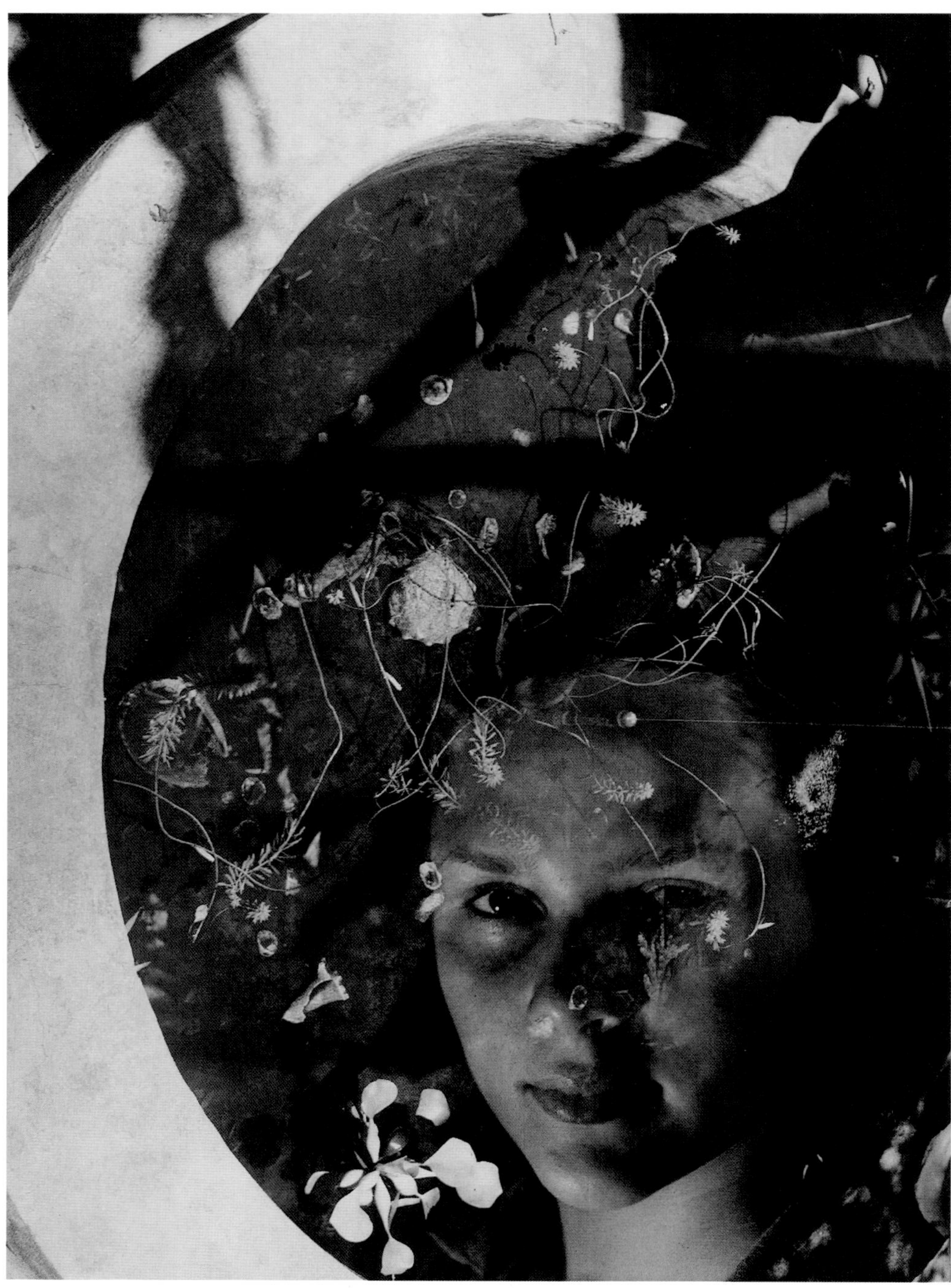

THE MAGIC POOL
1939

Clarence John Laughlin to Weeks Hall, October 27, 1941

Of course I am fully aware that my peculiar type of imagination will never fully externalize itself in studio fashion work.

Opposite:
WOMAN REFLECTED IN A MIRROR
1938

"Ideas for Photographs" (1937), handwritten note

Use mirrors and metal plates to spread reflected light onto portions of objects.

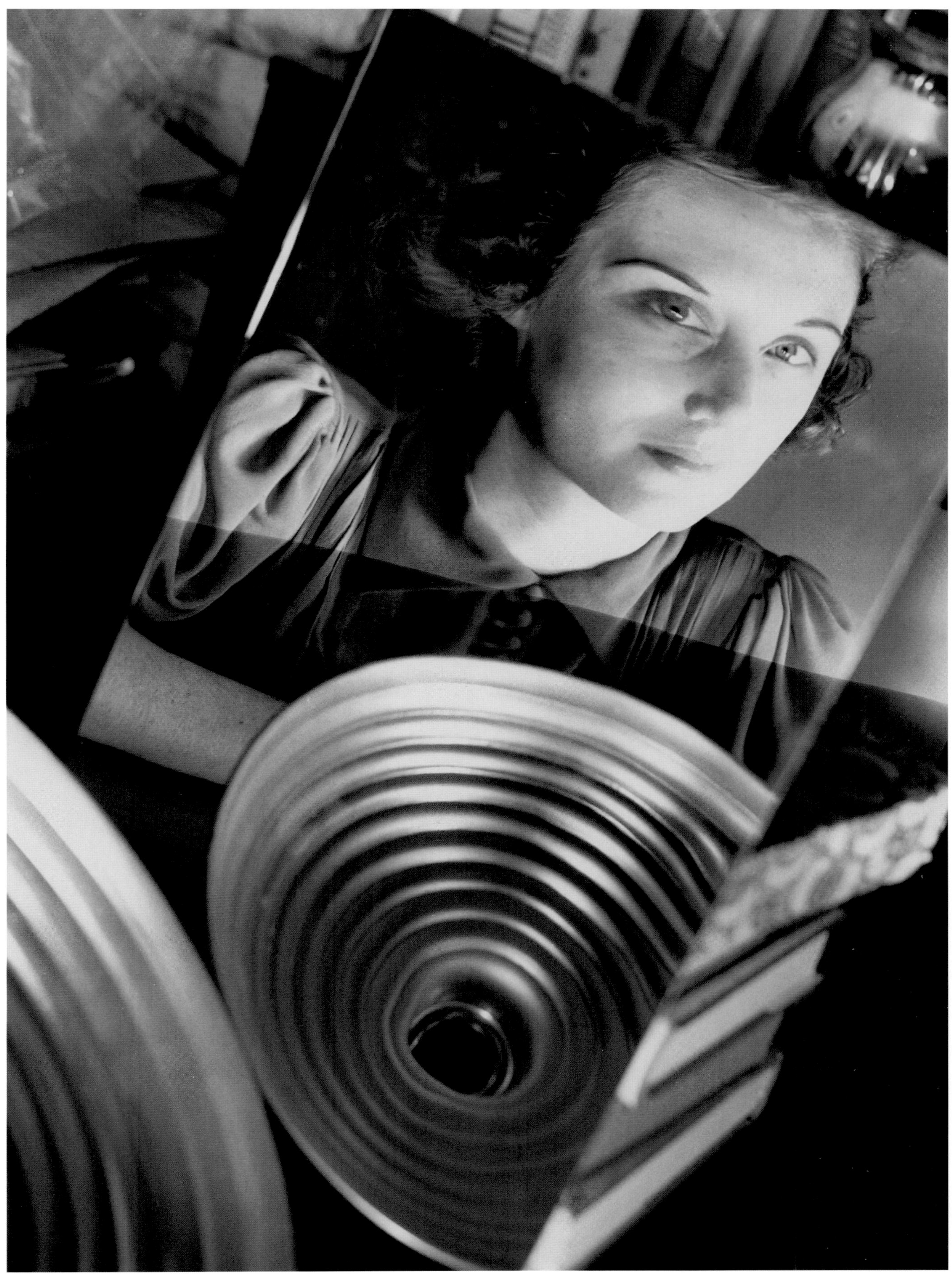

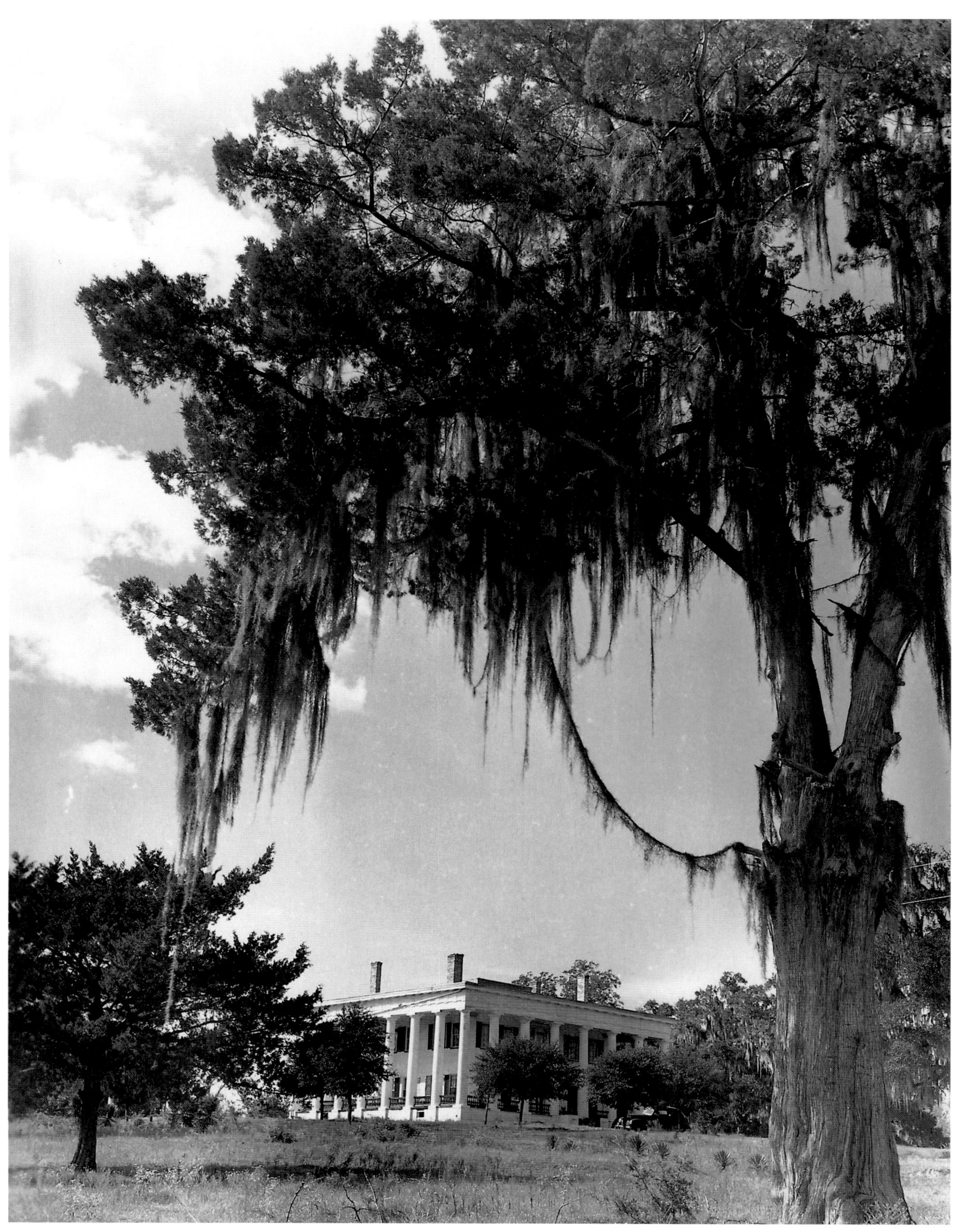

Memory, Mint Juleps, and My Grandfather

SHIRLEY ANN GRAU

Opposite:
UNDER LOOPS OF MOSS
1940

Ghosts Along the Mississippi *(New York: Scribner's, 1948)*

The dark mystery of time, the luminous and lingering mystery of light are the chief protagonists on the darkening stage occupied by the last structures of the doomed plantation system.

Memory, my grandfather used to say, is a most amazing thing. It is what makes a human being human. It is what links one generation to another. Common memories are the cement of civilization.

Whenever he began talking like that, it meant that he was about to launch into one of his long disquisitions. (Tirades, my grandmother called them; ruminative soliloquies, he said.) He first poured himself a highball, added sugar until there was a half inch deposit on the bottom of the glass. Then he went into the kitchen garden to pick a long sprig of mint for top garnish. If it was late in the year, if there had been a hard frost and the mint had shriveled or vanished completely, he would stand contemplatively for a few minutes, stubbing at the clump with his toe. "I will keep this under glass next year." He never did, of course. He never even thought of it again until the next time he wanted a fragrant green decoration.

Anyway, there was no room in his small greenhouse. It was jammed — bench, shelf, floor, and even ceiling — with horticultural enthusiasms. There was a special kumquat bush, as stubby and round as a fat man. And an eight-foot-tall avocado tree grown from a pit. It was pruned every year and then hauled out into the summer sun by a sweating three-man crew; it actually did produce fruit, hard and dry and quite inedible. A bougainvillea vine, leggy and thorny with occasional raggedy clusters of brilliant pink flowers, dangled from the rafters overhead. And all the small pots — row on row of scrawny plants, dozens and dozens of them, the waifs and strays of the botanical world. My grandfather's lifelong ambition was to discover an unknown species, some bit of green that would carry his name into the obscure lists in reference books. The pursuit of that dream led him to search the corners of old pastures and the kudzu-covered chimneys of burned-out farmhouses, even litter-filled city lots. The cuttings and clippings, the seeds and bulbs, and corms and rhizomes all came into his greenhouse, to be housed in neat numbered rows and inspected carefully, if sporadically. They were all failures; not one proved a suitable vehicle for his immortality. Most sulked and dwindled in their pots until they were finally swept away by one of the periodic epidemics of insects or virus that swept through the small space. "I am," he declared loudly to anyone who would listen, "a magician. For me plants grow back into the ground and disappear. . . ."

One small compact yellow iris showed brilliant yellow flowers, but it was soon identified as a well-known wild variety. A mysterious shoot of rosebush from an abandoned garden sulked for three years before producing the blooms that identified it as Lady Banksia. Not in the least discouraged, he went on searching. And, of course, year after year he forgot to pot his own garden's mint for wintering over. The great power of human memory that he extolled so eloquently did not include such small homey housekeeping details.

Faced with the complete absence of mint, my grandfather shrugged and lifted his eyes to the sky, dramatically, a man in despair. On one such occasion, he spotted me watching him. He beckoned me over and delivered to a bewildered ten-year-old a complicated explanation of the concept of Tyche, or Fate, among the ancient Greeks. I didn't understand a single word, but I was immensely flattered.

Slowly, ponderously, with the air of an elephant moving through the brush, my grandfather left the herb garden for the house, the kitchen, and the refrigerator.

A refrigerator, not an icebox. A mechanical marvel that was his pride and joy, a yellowish bowlegged structure with a condenser coil like a crown on top, that wheezed and purred and produced strange-tasting air-bubble-flecked ice cubes.

(My grandmother still kept an icebox, large and sleek and newly purchased from Sears, on the back porch. The iceman still came twice a week to slip his heavy burlap-wrapped block into the upper compartment. He stayed for a moment or two, foot propped on the top step, to tell my grandmother the latest neighborhood gossip, while she gave him her selections for the day's horse racing at various tracks around the country. He placed the bets with a mysterious bookie known only as Mr. Andrew.)

My grandfather ignored the icebox, went straight to the refrigerator, and checked the contents carefully, as if he expected a bunch of mint to appear miraculously. Finally, with a deep theatrical sigh, he removed a sprig of parsley from the bunch that was always kept, wrapped in a damp cloth, on the second shelf. He then tucked the long-stemmed bit of green into his drink, adjusted the angle to the proper rakish tilt. He was ready.

He settled himself on the front porch, in a cane rocker specially made to accommodate his long legs. Chairside there was a low round table on which my grandmother kept a small bunch of flowers or a sweet potato vine or a bit of ivy. Whatever it was, my grandfather always put it on the floor, carelessly, not caring if trailing vines were crushed under the rockers. He rode his chair hard, feet crashing down each time, chair moving

Opposite:
SUNBURSTS
1939

Weeks Hall to Clarence John Laughlin, September 19, 1941

The ace in the hole of black-and-white photography has been the rendering of texture. The mind rejects repetition, and the weather-worn forms of nature have an automatically pleasing variableness, within order, which photographs with usually certain results. I can quite assure you that the Greyhound bus station on Canal Street will, a hundred years from now, look, in a photograph, better than Saenger's [Theater] in that time. Restore both, and the bus station will still look better. It is better. Quality is inherent in itself. Competent restoration is like competent photography, but the layman has no time for the difference, as we know.

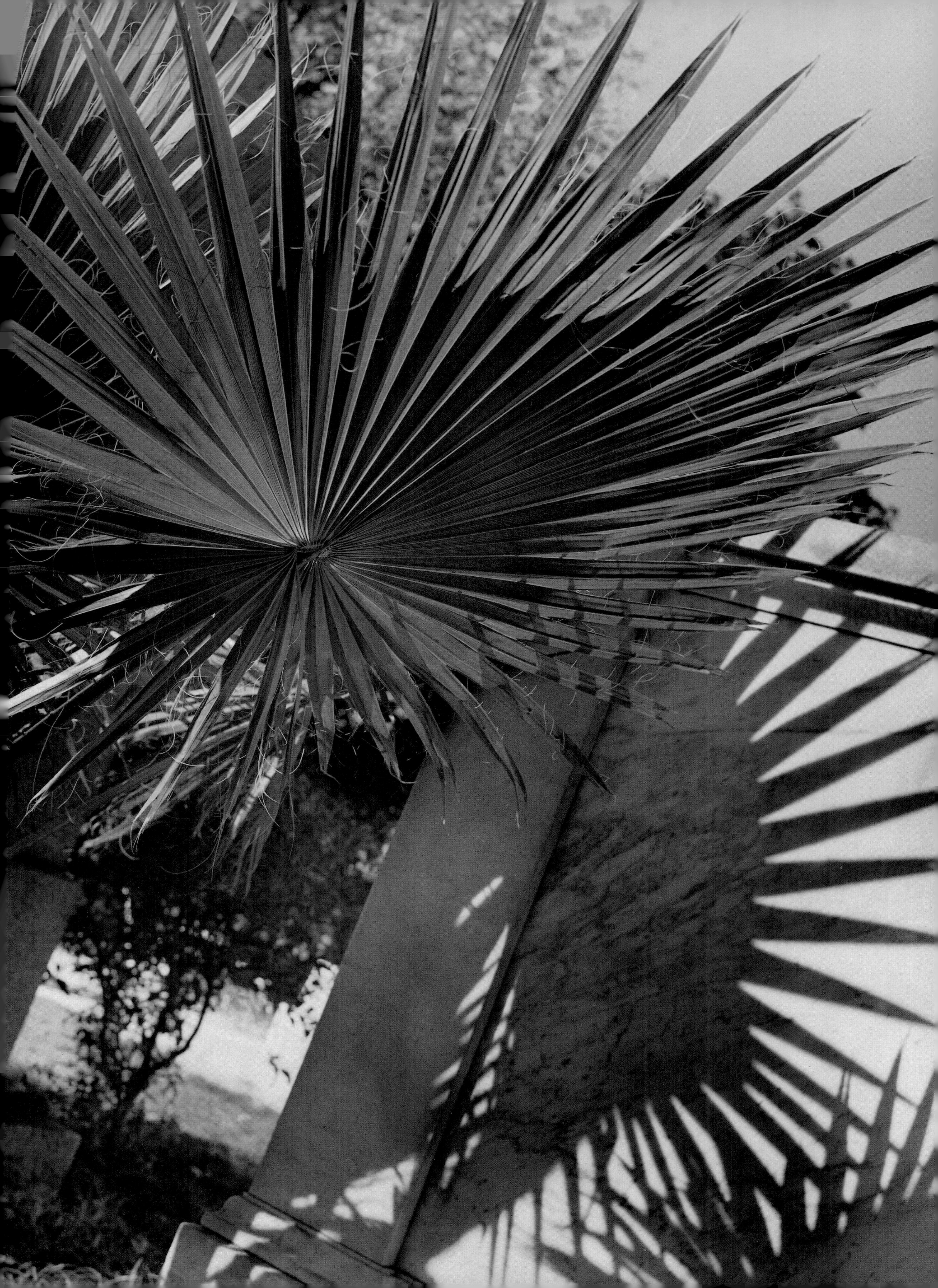

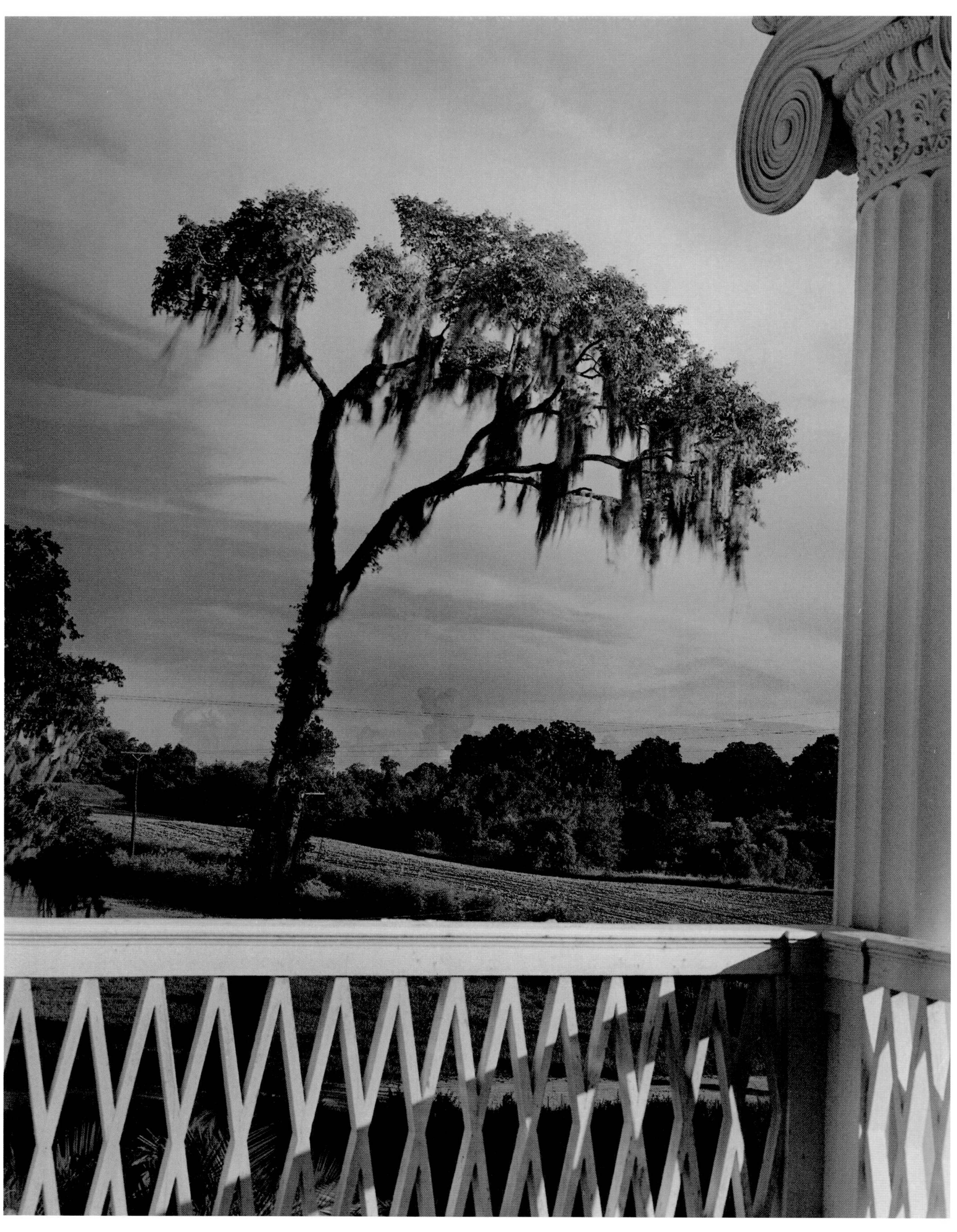

across the porch as if it had wheels. He'd worn tracks into the floor; they crisscrossed back and forth across the gray painted boards.

There, whatever the weather, in his chair on his porch, he had his drink — toddy, he called it. (And the glass, he insisted, was a proper toddy glass, from Ireland.) In cold months the porch was enclosed by an elaborate set of hinged windows, awkward heavy panels that took several days to install. During warm weather those panels were stored under the house in neat three-deep piles. There was plenty of room for them there — it was an old-fashioned house, built high off the ground. Its dim sheltered spaces provided convenient storage for adults. For children the entire area was a mysterious playground, cool in summer, cold in winter, smelling always of the heavy rich sweet earth. In summer my cats and dogs and I explored the tangled jumble of pipes and wiring and hid out, bandits in our secret cave, to watch the feet of passersby. In winter sacks of oysters were kept there, and bags of potatoes and onions. And once, weeks before Christmas, I found my special present: a red and silver two-wheel bike, partially assembled, still in its box.

After a few moments the rocking slowed. The chair had moved itself next to the porch rail, the glass with its garnish of mint or parsley was half empty. And the neighborhood children had arrived. There were always six or eight of them, more during summer vacation, most of all during the Christmas holidays. Boys and girls ready to hear a story.

He always started the same way, with a question. "Answer me this. When you young people came up the front steps a minute ago, you walked right by a cat. What color was he? Don't anybody turn around. . . . You didn't notice? Well then, what color is this house painted? No, it's not gray. You're just guessing because you don't know. I ought to send you home. . . . If you can't remember, how do you know you've been here? Maybe you aren't here. Think of that. Maybe you're not sitting on this porch, maybe you didn't come up the steps past the cat. Maybe this house isn't here at all. If you don't remember, you might just as well stay home, stay in bed, because you aren't really seeing anything or thinking anything or being anywhere."

Then, warmed by his own peroration, he began to tell stories. He had the diction of an old-fashioned Shakespearean actor. (Some of the children thought he had come from a distant, exotic place, so artificial were those dulcet voice tones.) His whispers could be heard down the block, his shouts shook the pigeons from their roosts under the eaves.

They were good stories; they were wonderful stories. They were filled with action and adventure, with daring exploits and hairbreadth escapes. And they were always told in the first person.

He was a good actor. He made us children hear the creak of the timbers on the *Mayflower*, smell the stench of the bilge, shudder at the first sight of the low gray empty coast. . . . Or he'd tell of a Mormon family,

Opposite:
ENCHANTED TREE, NUMBER ONE
1947

Clarence John Laughlin's caption

The tree seems magically suspended in the afternoon sky, and might easily have appeared in a canvas of Claude Lorrain. The landscape expresses something of the flatness and lushness of Louisiana's terrain.

Utah-bound by wagon train from Missouri to a winter spent in a sod house and a plague of snakes in the spring. . . . Or he'd become a sea captain encountering a ghost ship on a stormy night off Cape Hatteras. . . . In a flash he might change into Paul Bunyan or Alligator Joe and set us laughing with his outrageous bragging tall tales. . . . Sometimes he sang lilting Irish songs with endless verses and a cheerful "Singsong Kitty" refrain. Other times his songs were those of a black man working on the Ohio River, calling on the morning star to witness his endless labor. . . .

The afternoon raced past. It was suppertime, mothers were calling children home, some by name, some by a clapping of hands, one by loud blasts on a police whistle. The children vanished as quietly and as quickly as they had arrived. My grandfather pulled a spoon from his vest pocket and began eating the sugar from the bottom of his toddy glass. From the dining room behind us came a clatter of china, rattle of silverware, small chink of ice in glasses. In its timely, well-ordered fashion, the day was ending. All up and down the street windows were turning blank reflections to the setting sun. A sad time, the way all endings are sad.

"Are the stories true?" I'd always ask.

"All stories are true," my grandfather said, "if you believe them."

"I'll remember them," I promised.

"Of course you will," he said.

Opposite:

A CANOPY OF GREEN, NUMBER ONE

1939

Fritz Gruber, "Clarence John Laughlin: A Mystic of the Camera," Photo-Prisma *(February 1960), typescript translation by Dr. Eric Albrecht*

The past . . . breathes in his photographs where he has sought out the old, fallen, and forgotten mansions of Louisiana and preserved them in their poignant decay.

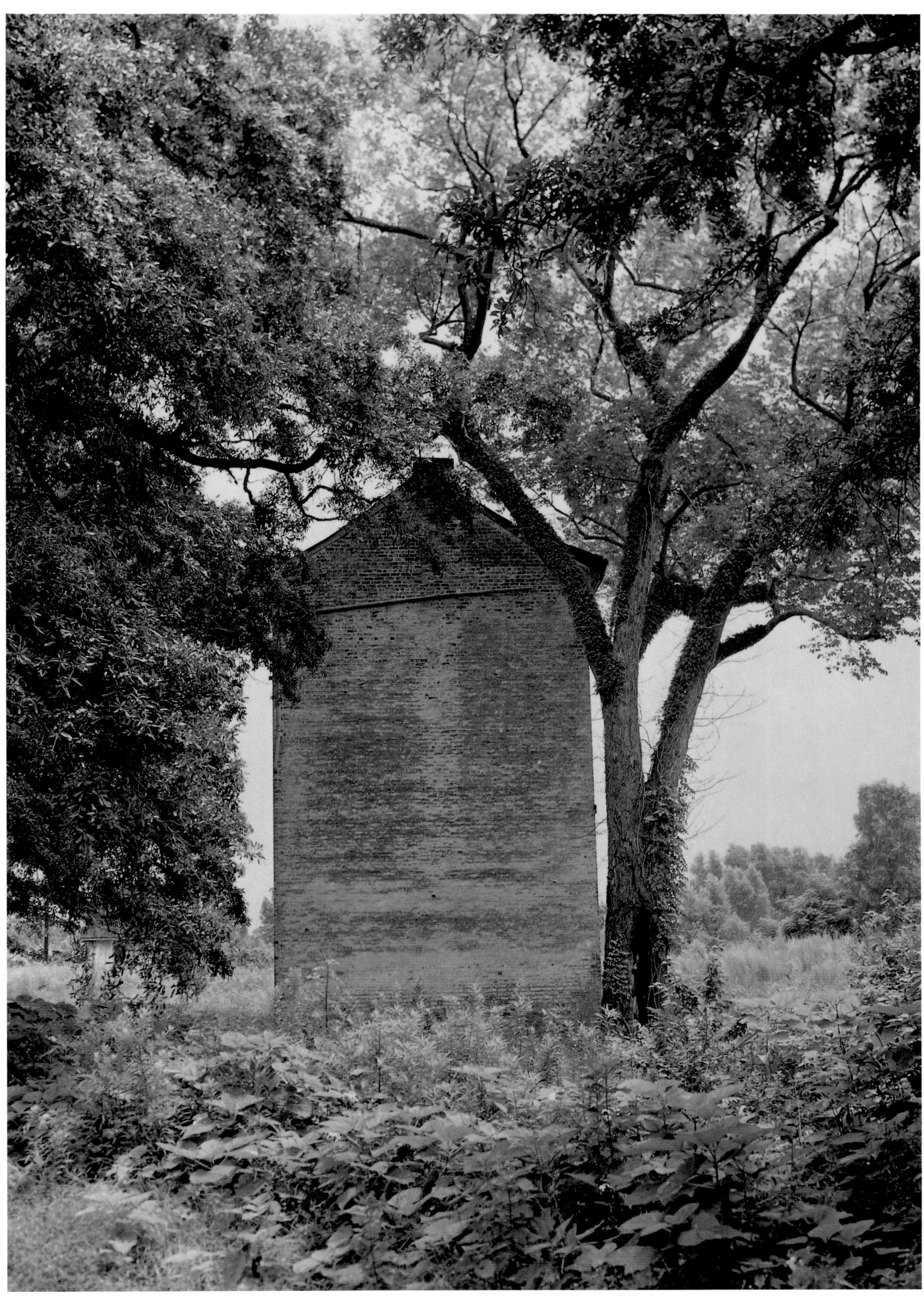

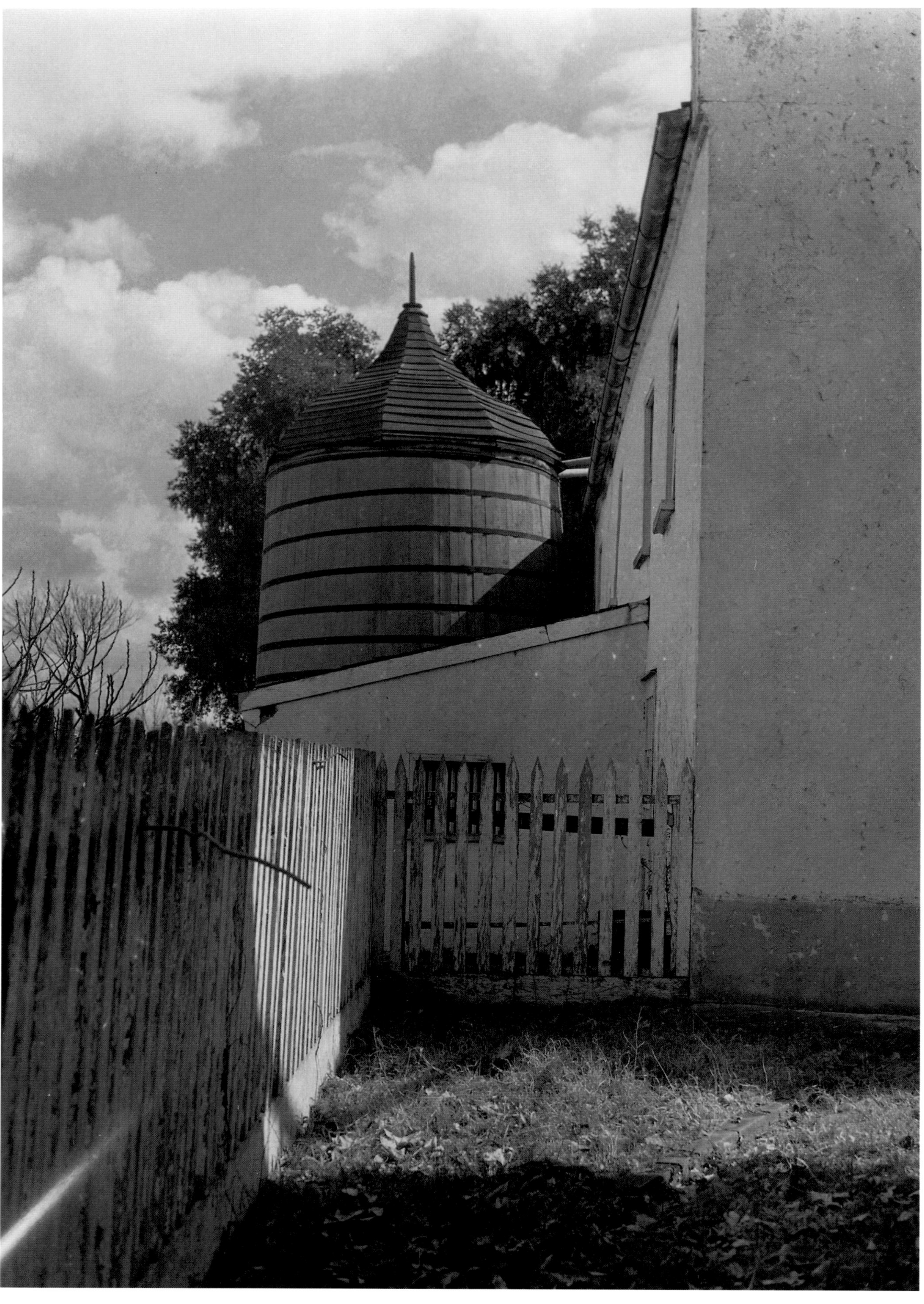

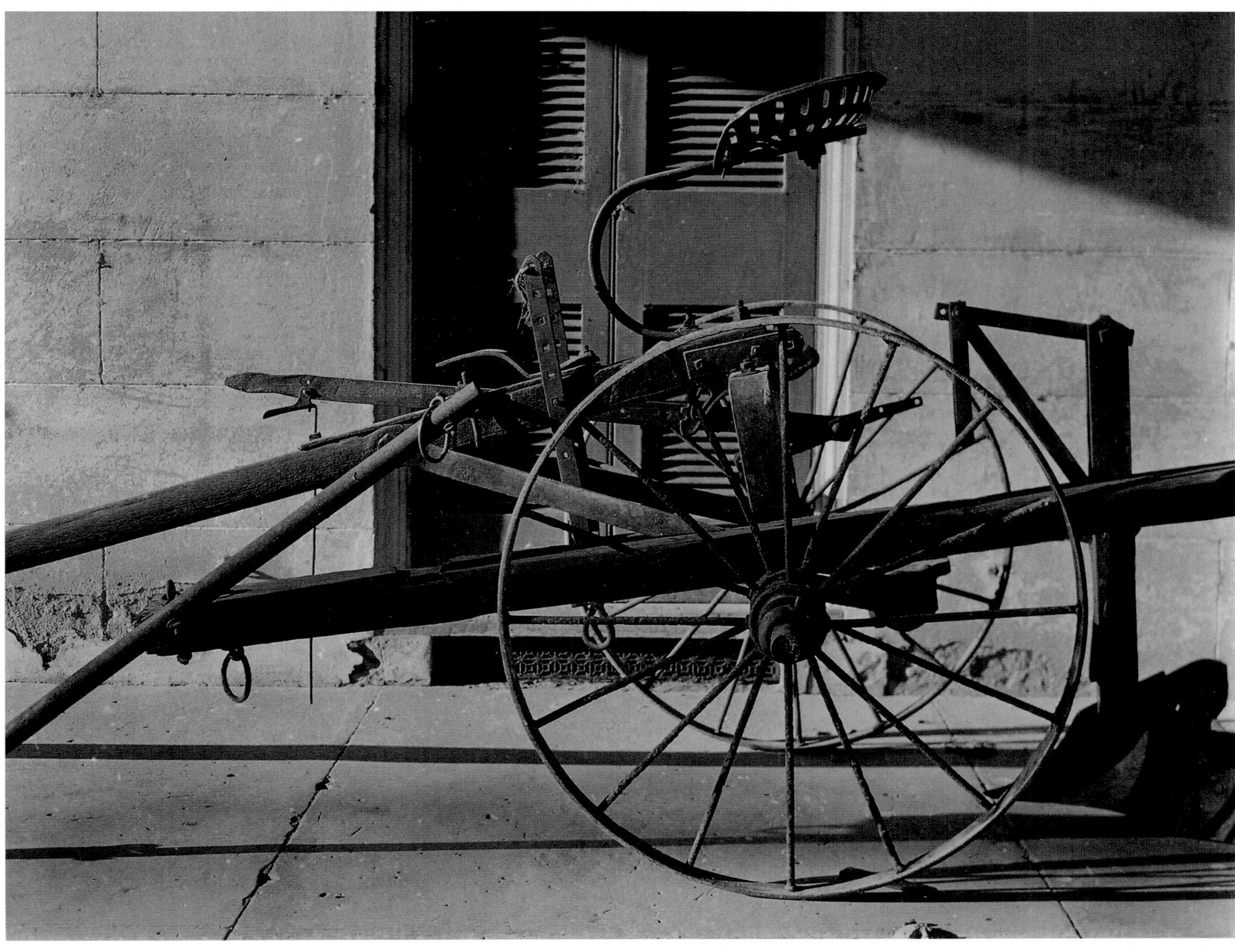

Opposite:
NEAR BURNSIDE, LOUISIANA
1938

Clarence John Laughlin to Eugene Berman, December 12, 1940

I want to do a series of pictures of old Louisiana towns — there is some marvelous material in them.

ONLY THE RIVER NOW PLOUGHS THE FIELDS
1938

"Romantic Visions" (1983), typescript

[My work] rises from an inherent tendency toward what might be called "animism." . . . And thus, instead of dealing with the object as a thing-in-itself, to deal with it as a thing-beyond-itself.

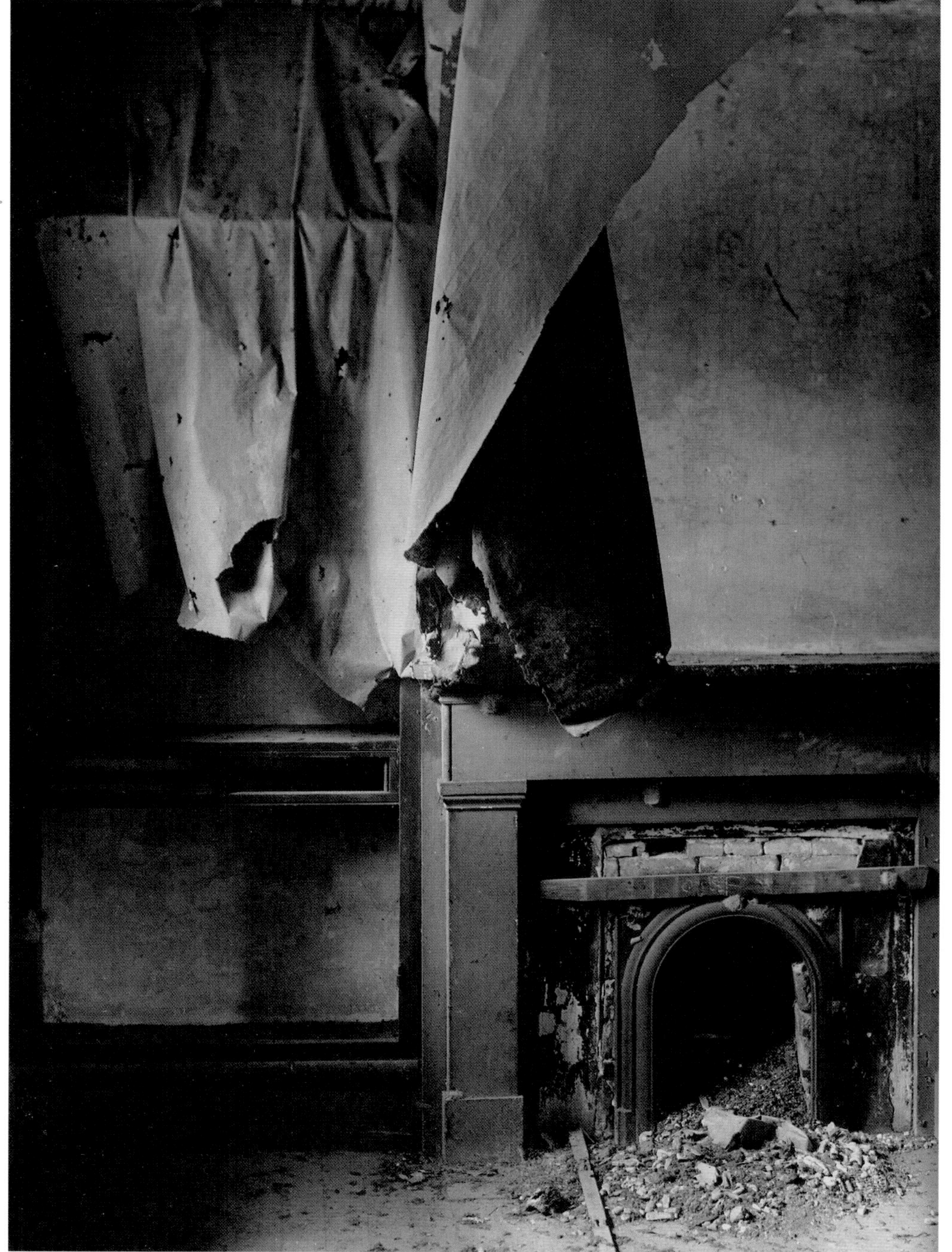

Opposite:
"CAJUN" GIRLS
1941

James Laughlin to Clarence John Laughlin, July 1944

The photographs are stunning. Wonderful light and textures in them.

THE ROOM OF SHROUDS
1939

Clarence John Laughlin to Man Ray, May 20, 1941

I quite agree with you that the photographer who produces a photograph which is merely technically good, owes more to the discoveries of the laboratory technicians than to himself. However, the imagination transcends all technical perfection, and sometimes even converts a technical disadvantage into a further success.

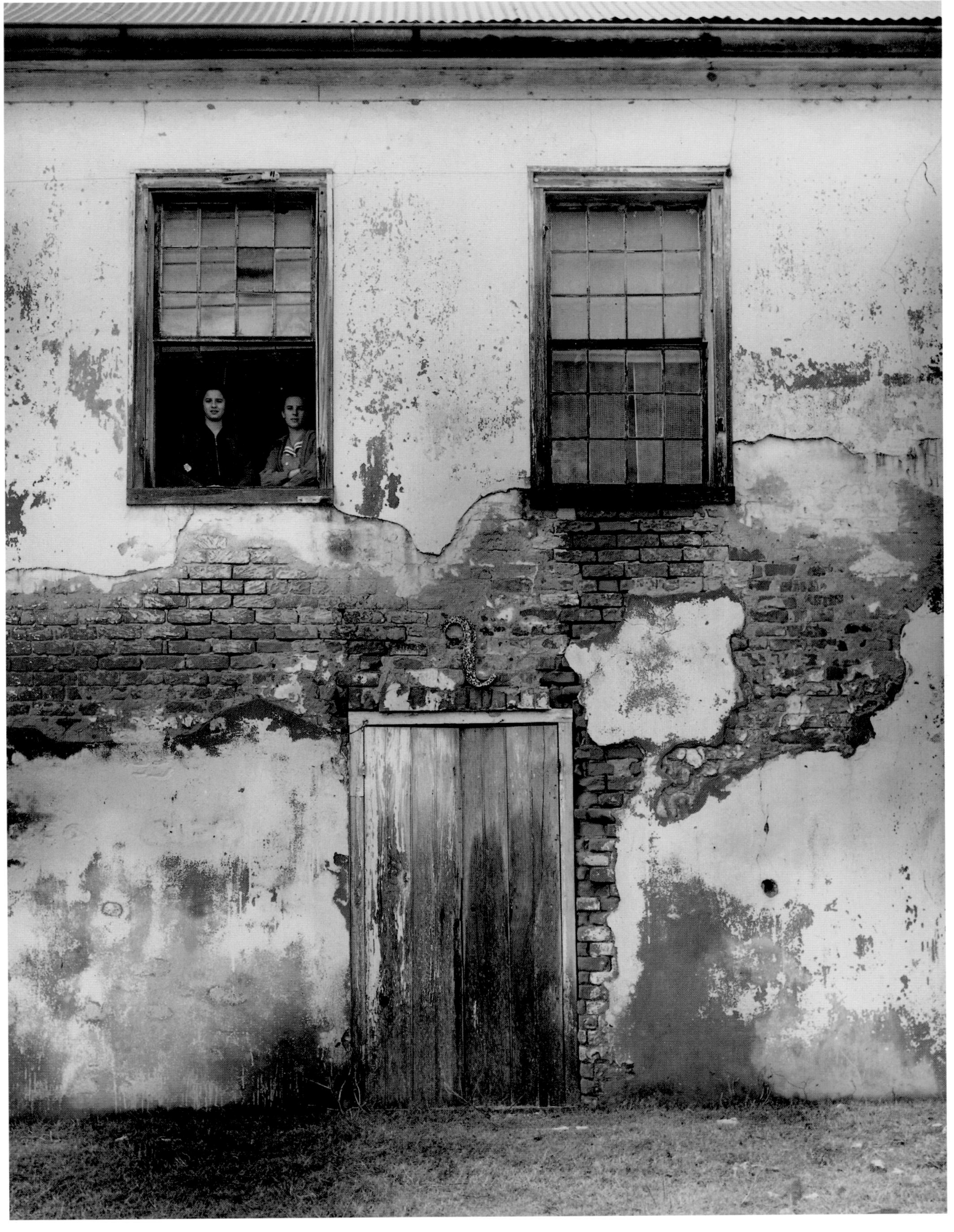

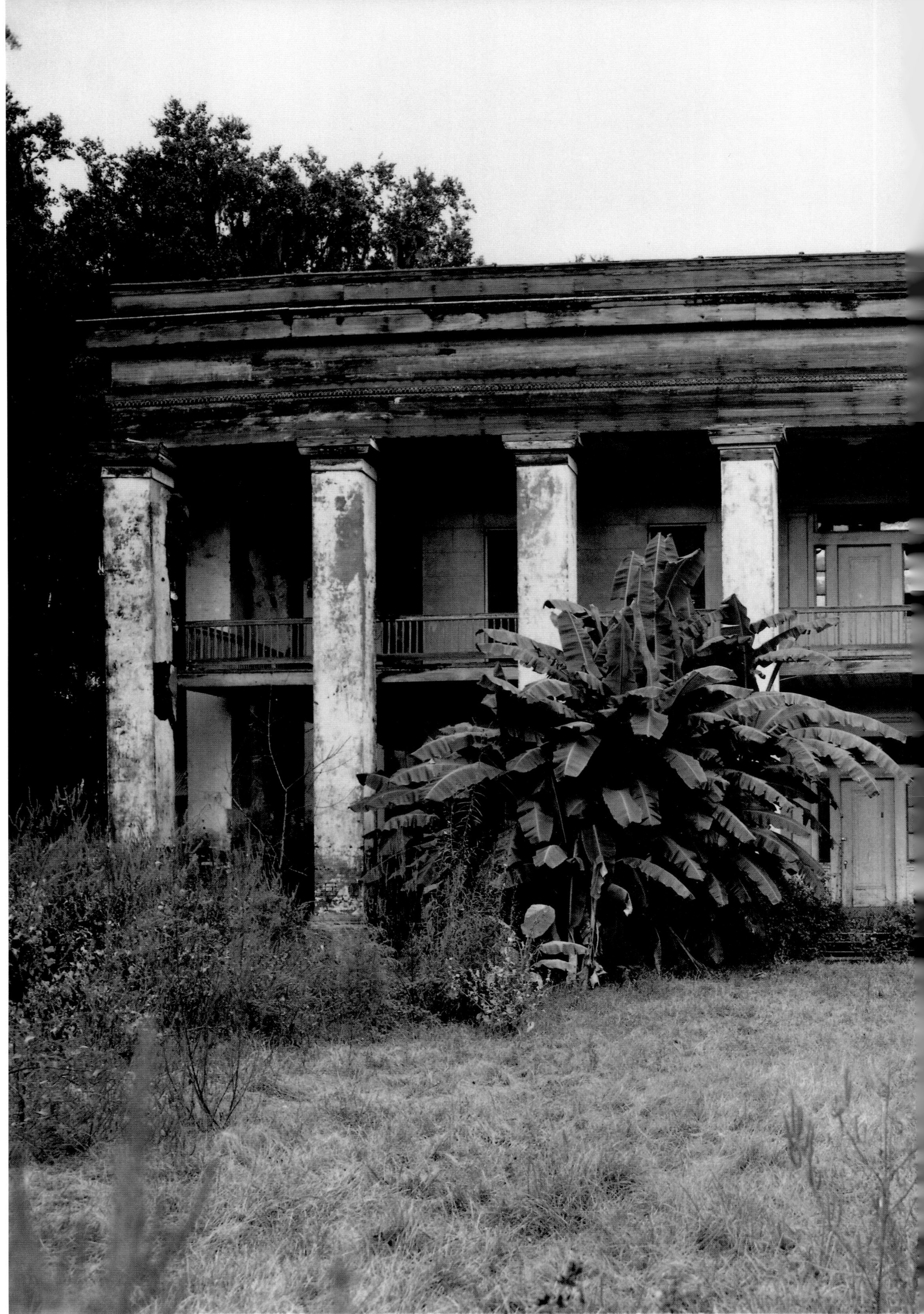

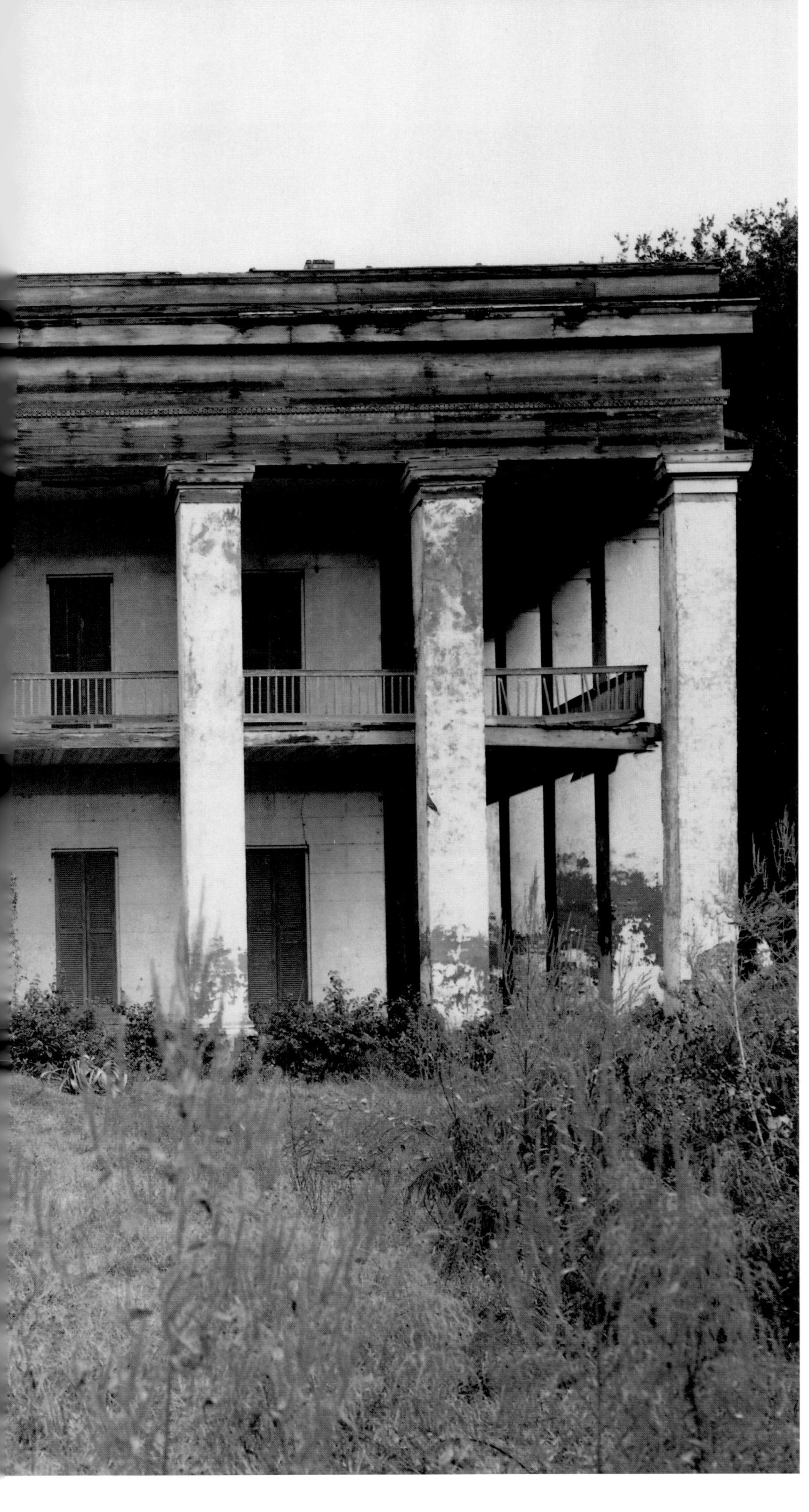

THE MIGHTY PILLARS, NUMBER FOUR

1939

Clarence John Laughlin to Eugene Berman, July 13, 1941

I have recently gone out to Ashland Plantation . . . only to find that even the enormous house is almost lost in a gigantic outburst of plant life.

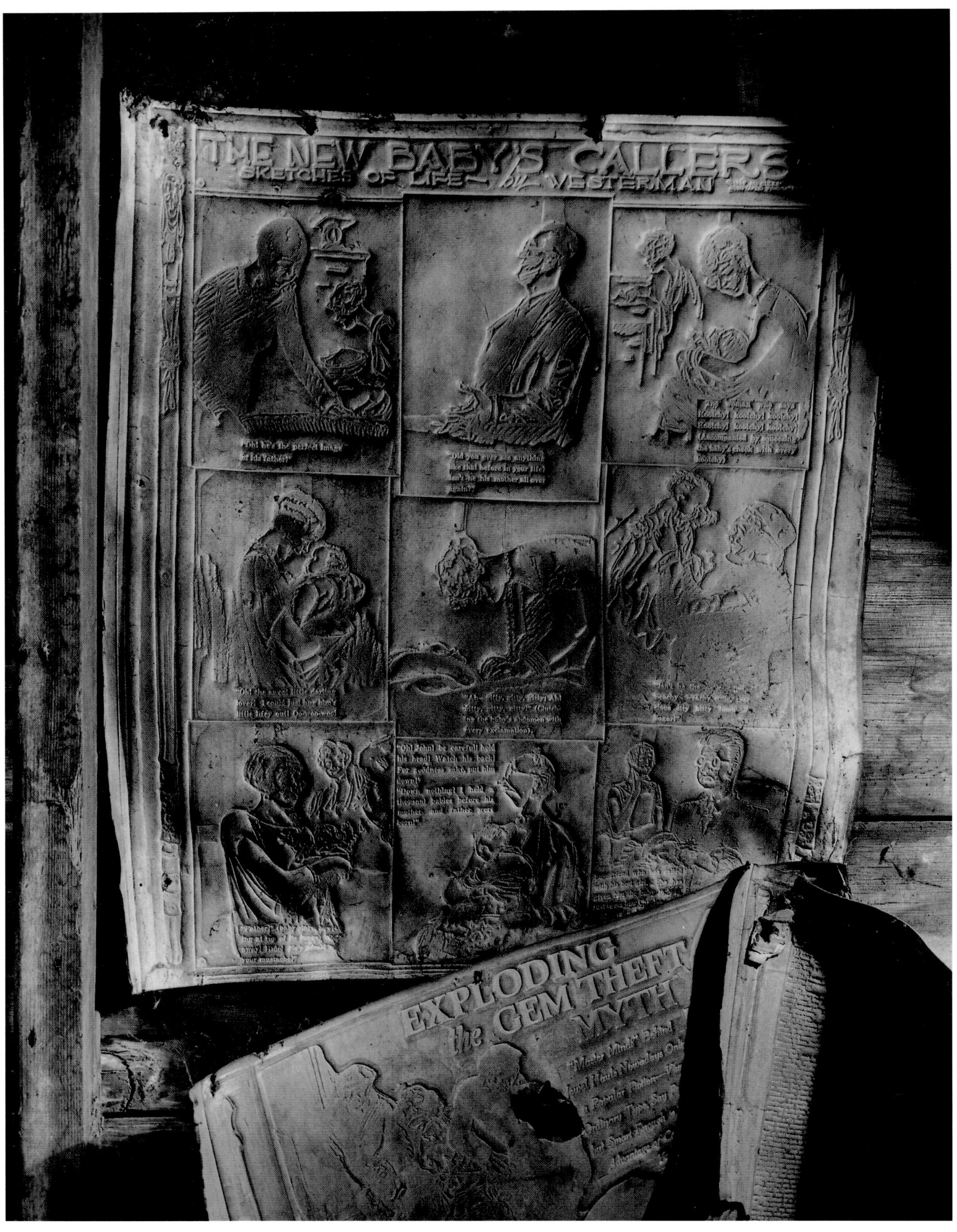

THE NEW BABY'S CALLERS
SKETCHES OF LIFE by WESTERMAN
EXPLODING the GEM THEFT MYTH

An Astonished Eye Looks Out of the Air

JONATHAN WILLIAMS

Opposite:
THE NEW BABY'S CALLERS MEET THE EXPLODED GEM THIEF
1954

Clarence John Laughlin to Weeks Hall, August 8, 1941

It infuriates me to see people with the power and position . . . try to stem the development of symbolic or hyper-real photography, and to force conformity upon all photographers.

Way down yonder in New Orleans, back in the Days when de Lawd walked the Earth jes like a Natchrul Man, and everything in God's Creation was bright-eyed, bushy-tailed, and wet behind the ears, Proteus came up the Mississippi and started taking photographs. He called himself All Eyes, but his real name was Clarence John Laughlin. Who needs LSD when you can drop CJL into your mind's eye? *Phantasmagoric* beats *lysergic* any day. Clarence was born in the days when Southern children were dosed with paregoric and Coca-Cola syrup for the colic; and people would go into the soda fountain and say, "Honey, gimme a dope." (Coca-Cola had more punch in those days.) But CJL didn't just want a Coke, or a Coke Float, or a Lemon Coke, or even a Cherry Coke; he wanted Coke with a little nepenthe thrown in. Maybe even a dash of ichor.

What a shape-shifter was All Eyes. Writing about him again after all this time (I met him thirty-five years ago), my usual laconic Appalachian style wants to do some flailing about, with more than a little heavy-duty fustigating. Maybe I should call on George Lewis's rhythm section (Lawrence Marrero, banjo; Alcide "Slow Drag" Pavageau, bass; Joe Watkins, drums) to settle me down? Not that those great New Orleans musicians ever settled CJL down.

He was always "too much pork for just one fork." He was a catbird. He was hot to trot. He rambled all around, in and out of the town. He was a sight and a half. He saw "things." He was a phantast. He was Mr. Eye-Magination. He could animate a frozen turnip. He was the pixilated, pileated voice of Woody Woodpecker. He was an eidolon, a three-lobed burning eye that "frothed in primal slime at the center of nuclear chaos" (right in there with another master of tasteful restraint, Mr. H. P. Lovecraft). He was cosmodemonic, psychopompous, and sometimes a jerk. He surely wore the pants off Old Proteus. He was definitely *too much!* And *how much* I miss him. Every time I encounter the Marvelous, in a place, in a person, in a book, in a building, in an object, I want to send a fax to CJL in the Elysian Fields and tell him about it. I would love to take him to meet some Southerners of his ilk that he never got to see and photograph: St. EOM of the Land of Pasaquan, Little Enis, Ralph Eugene Meatyard, Kay Du Vernet, Joni Mabe, Sweet Evening Breeze, Dilmus Hall, Henry Faulkner, James Harold Jennings, Georgia Blizzard, Howard Finster, Vollis Simpson, Mojo Nixon and the Toad Lickers, J. B. Murry, Royal Robertson — the list is much longer.

All Eyes was like Claude Monet, one of his masters, who told us: ". . . try to forget what objects you have before you, a tree, a house, a field or whatever." I'm sure that Clarence taught me as much about *seeing* language as much as Charles Olson, my own master, taught me about *hearing* words. When I started making poems in the 1950s, the South was full of amazing hand-painted signs. CJL showed me how to see what was there, as well as what wasn't there.

PEACHES HEAR

— a lovely little Taoist roadside poem by an orchard in Nacoochee Valley, Habersham County, Georgia.

O'NAN'S
AUTO
SERVICE

— the greatest "find" I have ever made, courtesy of the photographer Ralph Eugene Meatyard, who drove me to a mechanic's shop in the country north of Lexington, Kentucky. The Blue Grass was never the same after Gene finished with it. Who else would have found Lummy Jean Licklighter in the telephone book?

EAT!
300 FEET!

— which I titled "The Anthropophagites Get Down on a Barbecue Sign on Highway NC 107 South of Hamlet, North Carolina."

ANT
ON
BRUCKNER

— not a sign, but a small biomorphic discovery in the word itself, produced by using a bodacious and beady eye informed by Clarence John Laughlin. Thank you, Maestro!

But, back to CJL before I wander off over the hill. I am asked to comment on some rarities in his series "The Magic of the Object" (Series S in the CJL canon). These images are here prefaced by some of his early still lifes from the 1930s, before he started dividing the photographs up into twenty-three sacred categories. One statement, precisely, defines what he would do in this area for all his life: "Everything, everything, no matter

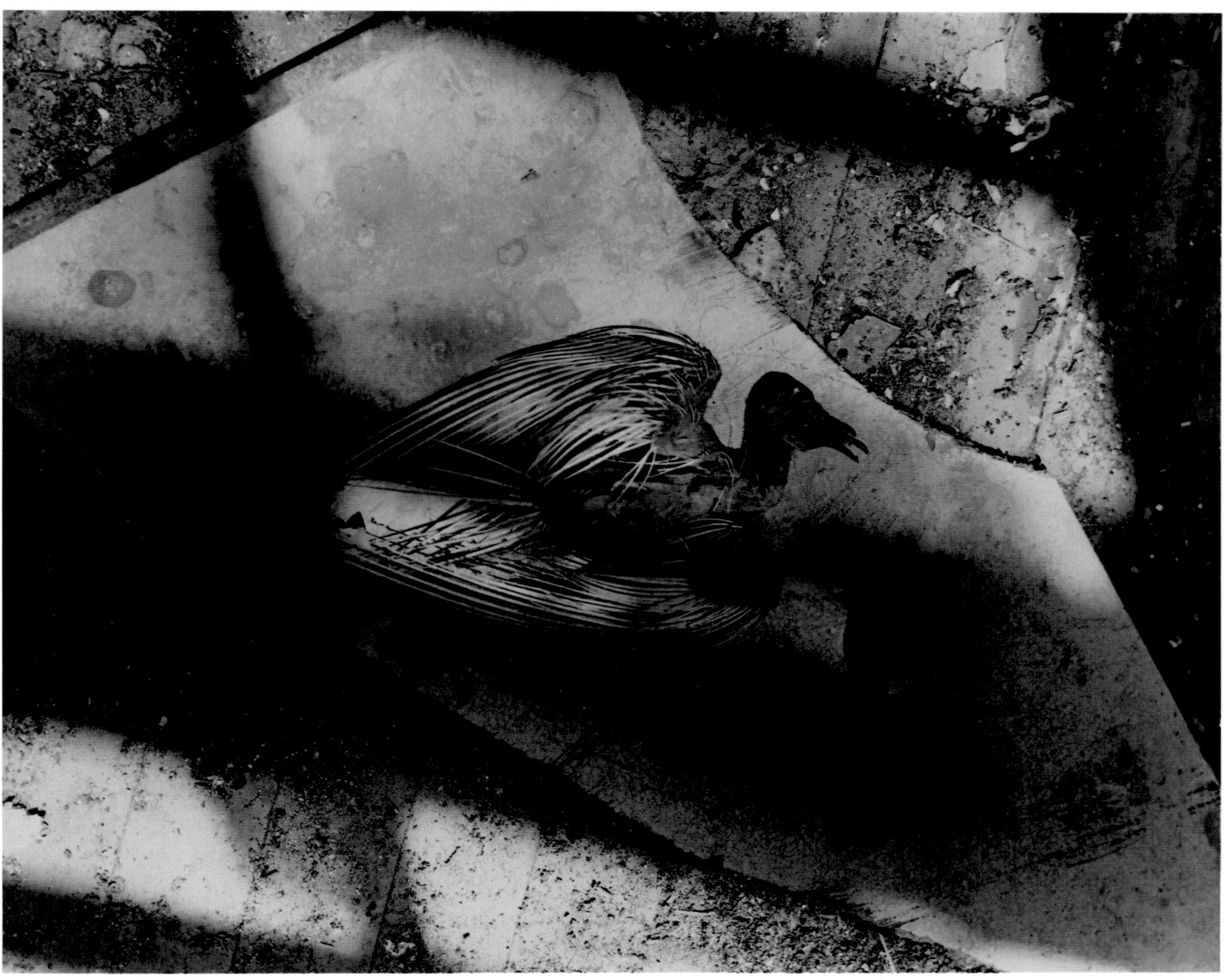

THE DESICCATED HEART, NUMBER ONE
1961

Clarence John Laughlin to Enid Foster, October 6, 1956

However, this much I know: dissatisfaction with one's self, and dissatisfaction with the world, is necessary — it is one of the prime things that keep the artist going on — that drives him — happiness, as such, must come in between times, as best it can.

how commonplace or how ugly, has secret meanings. Everything." Comment I will, chronologically, but whether I can evoke CJL's visionary, innermost-bird-of-the-inner-eye style is in question. All Eyes reckoned that all of us eyeless poor folks were blind as nineteen bats and dim as a sack full of buttholes.

(1) "The New Baby's Callers Meet the Exploded Gem Thief," abandoned house, Salt Lake City, Utah, 1954. Not quite kosher to juxtapose the texts of two old newspaper maquettes and then misquote them in cavalier, poetic fashion. But who's complaining? The magic here is in the light.

(2) "The Desiccated Heart, Number One," abandoned church, Austin, Texas, 1961. Take one dead pigeon and one illuminatus, and there you have it. Pause to wonder.

(3) "A Dream of Pearls," 1940 or 1941. A bit of fustian/flummery in the tradition of the Bard's "those are pearls that were his eyes." A superb image in words — not so hot in such a contrived visual set piece. CJL is hard for me to look at in this mode. The image reminds me of a New York

photographer, sedulously avoided by tasteful critics and historians, named Val Telberg. I'd venture a bet that CJL thought he was great, and he probably *is* much better than we know.

(4) "Negative, and Positive Space, Number One," abandoned wood house, Cripple Creek, Colorado, 1955. A fantastic image. How instructive it would be to see the subject shot by Aaron Siskind, Wynn Bullock, Frederick Sommer, Harry Callahan, Minor White, Edward Weston, Brassai, Raymond Moore. CJL always seemed to see "more" than the law allowed. So I catch myself fixating on a hound dog's profile resting on the window frame, while below a strange personage of Plantagenet lineage (Dame Edith Sitwell?) muses on the scene.

(5) "Portrait of an Old Shutter, Number One," Gaillard cottage group, New Orleans, 1938. Homage to the sculptor James Surls, of Splendora, Texas (though I doubt that CJL ever saw his work). A giant figure with a brick head and huge arms opens its heart to the photographer's personal eye.

(6) "The Imprisoned Landscape," wrecked car, grounds of orange grove plantation, 1954. A displacement as strange as any in the paintings of René Magritte. As CJL noted: "Instead of seeing a car in a landscape, we see a landscape in a car."

(7) "The Leaping Shark," old English car, San Antonio, Texas, 1961. "Full many a flower is born to blush unseen, and waste its sweetness on the desert air," as the poet says and sighs. Only CJL had both a nose for invisible flowers and an eye as beady as a metal shark's. If Stephen King ever runs out of nightmares, he'd better run quick to the Laughlin Archive.

(8) "Depth Beyond Depth," New Orleans still life, 1936. Flash Gordon and Dr. Zharkov get together on the Planet Mongo and drink a few cocktails in the gravity-free lounge of the *Starship Monteleone*. Their discussion ranges from H. G. Wells's *The Time Machine* to a recent volume of photography from the Bauhaus workshops and on to Man Ray's photographs in the current issue of *Vogue*.

(9) "Philodendron and Dotted Swiss," New Orleans still life, 1936. Looks very like a rayogram; or a photogram by Moholy-Nagy; or (almost) a photogenic drawing produced by Fox Talbot at Lacock Abbey in Wiltshire a hundred years earlier. (Talbot bragged that his house in the country was the first that was ever known "to draw its own picture.") The space is so dematerialized that maybe a Japanese calligrapher/poet made the whole thing up in the first place, before CJL's camera got there?

Nothing could capture Clarence John Laughlin better than these two lines by Theodore Roethke:

> The dead will not lie still,
> And things throw light on things.

Opposite:

A DREAM OF PEARLS

1940 or 1941

"Some Observations on the Functions of Photography" (1939), typescript for a lecture

And the objects that men call "real" are only symbols because they are merely parts of something not fully known or perceived.

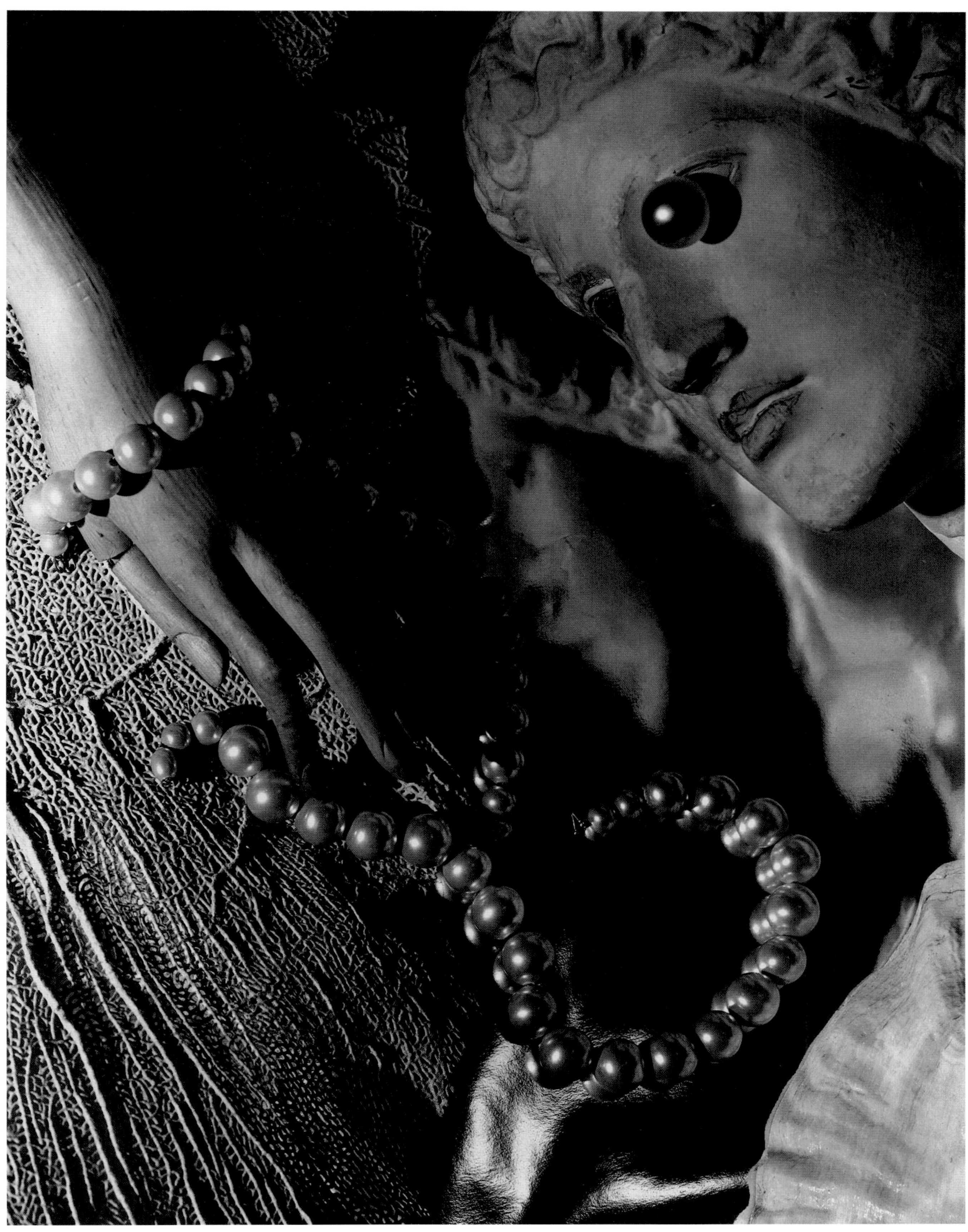

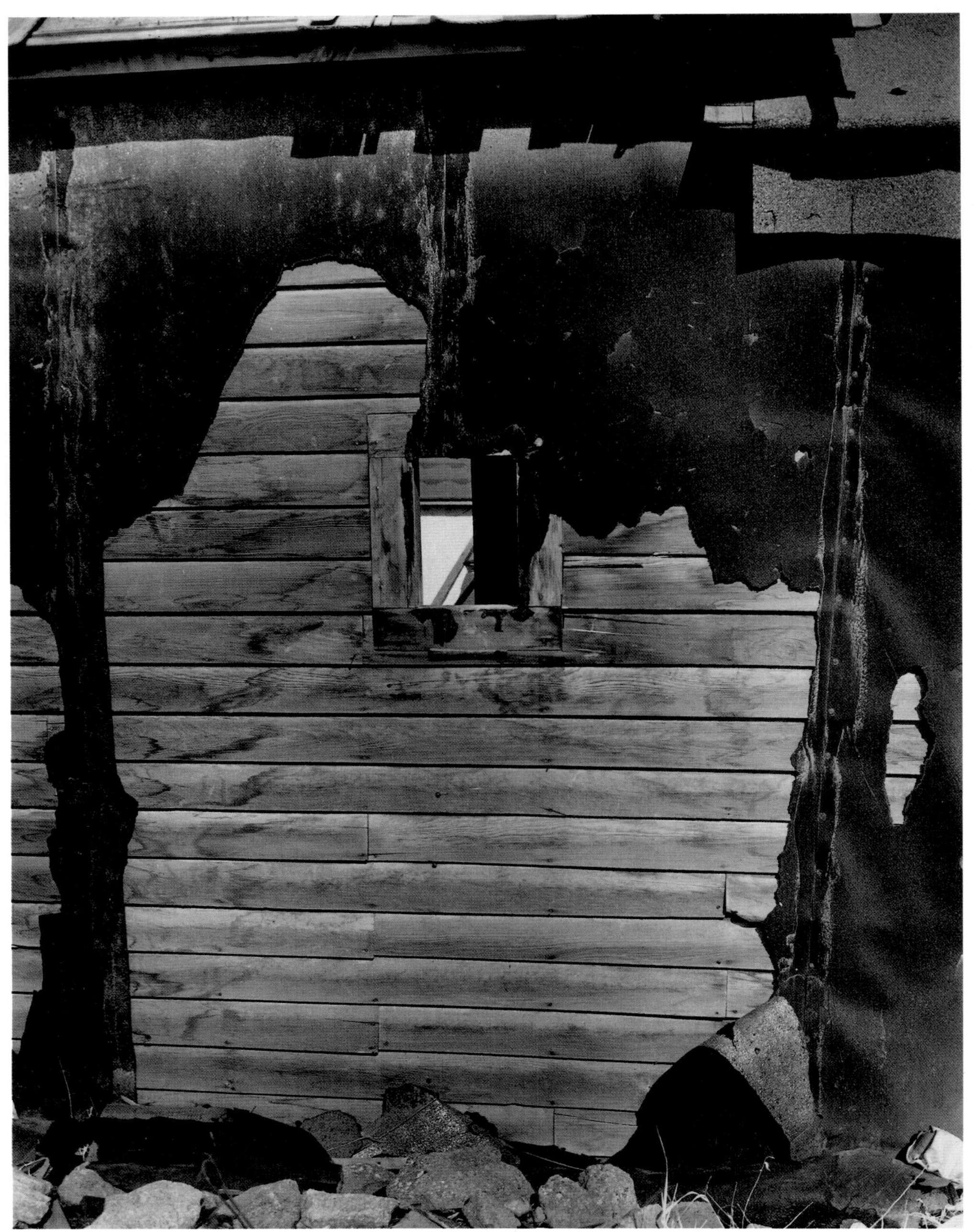

NEGATIVE, AND POSITIVE SPACE, NUMBER ONE
1955

"The Evolution of a Photographer" (1945), typescript

Between the cheap gibes of its detractors, the perversions and misuse [by] its own practitioners, the confusion and stupid solemnity of its "arty" friends who think it merely a handmaiden to bad painting, and the insensitive practicality of those who would relegate it chiefly to reporting, it is high time for the dignity of photography to be re-established.

Opposite:
PORTRAIT OF AN OLD SHUTTER, NUMBER ONE
1938

Clarence John Laughlin to Dorothy Norman, August 13, 1941

I could show you evidences of an amazing, and indigenous, kind of fantasy which sprang into being here, evidences which are to be found still, if they are carefully searched for, in the "lost" streets, the strange burial grounds, the impossibly decayed houses of old New Orleans.

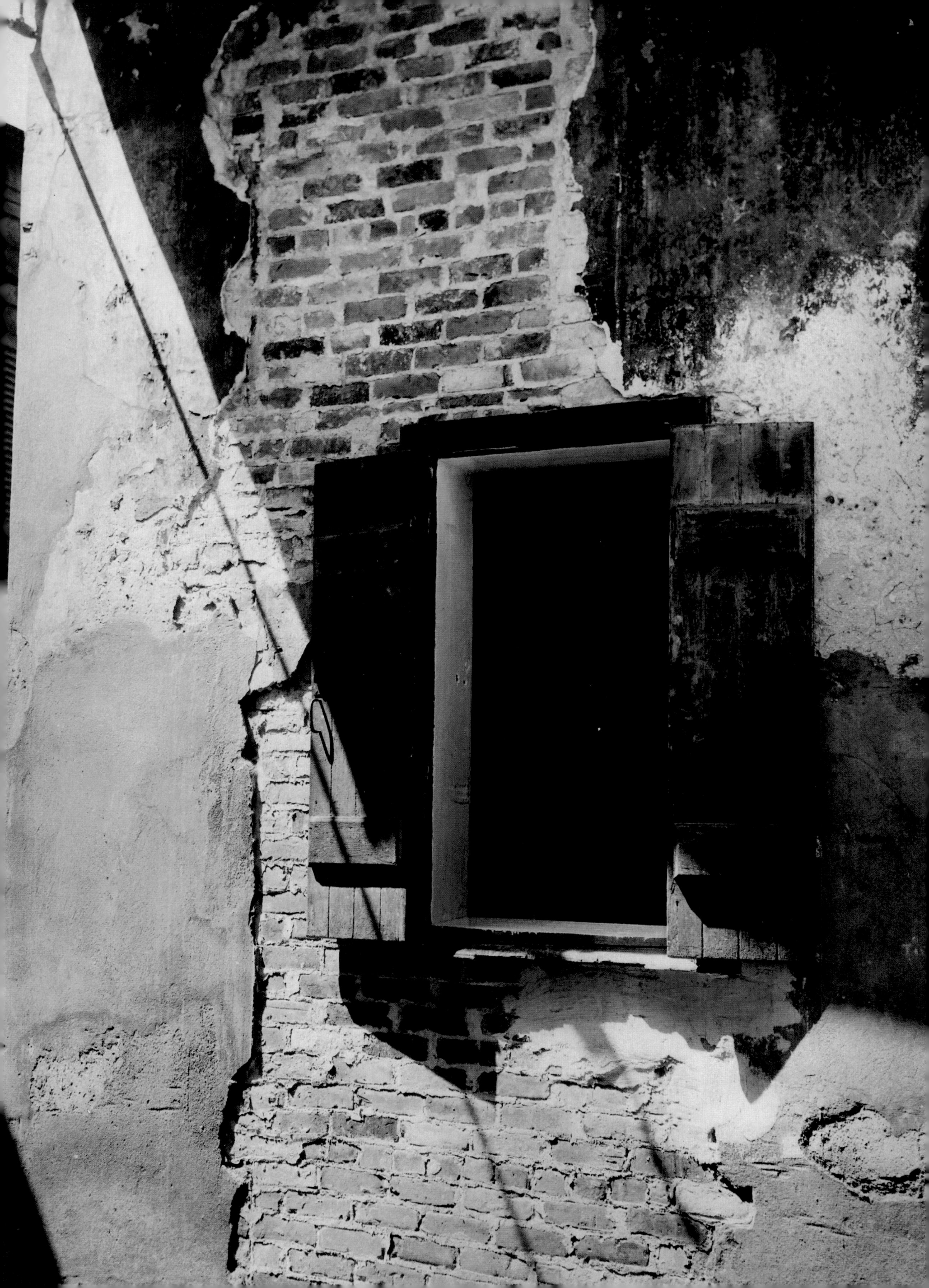

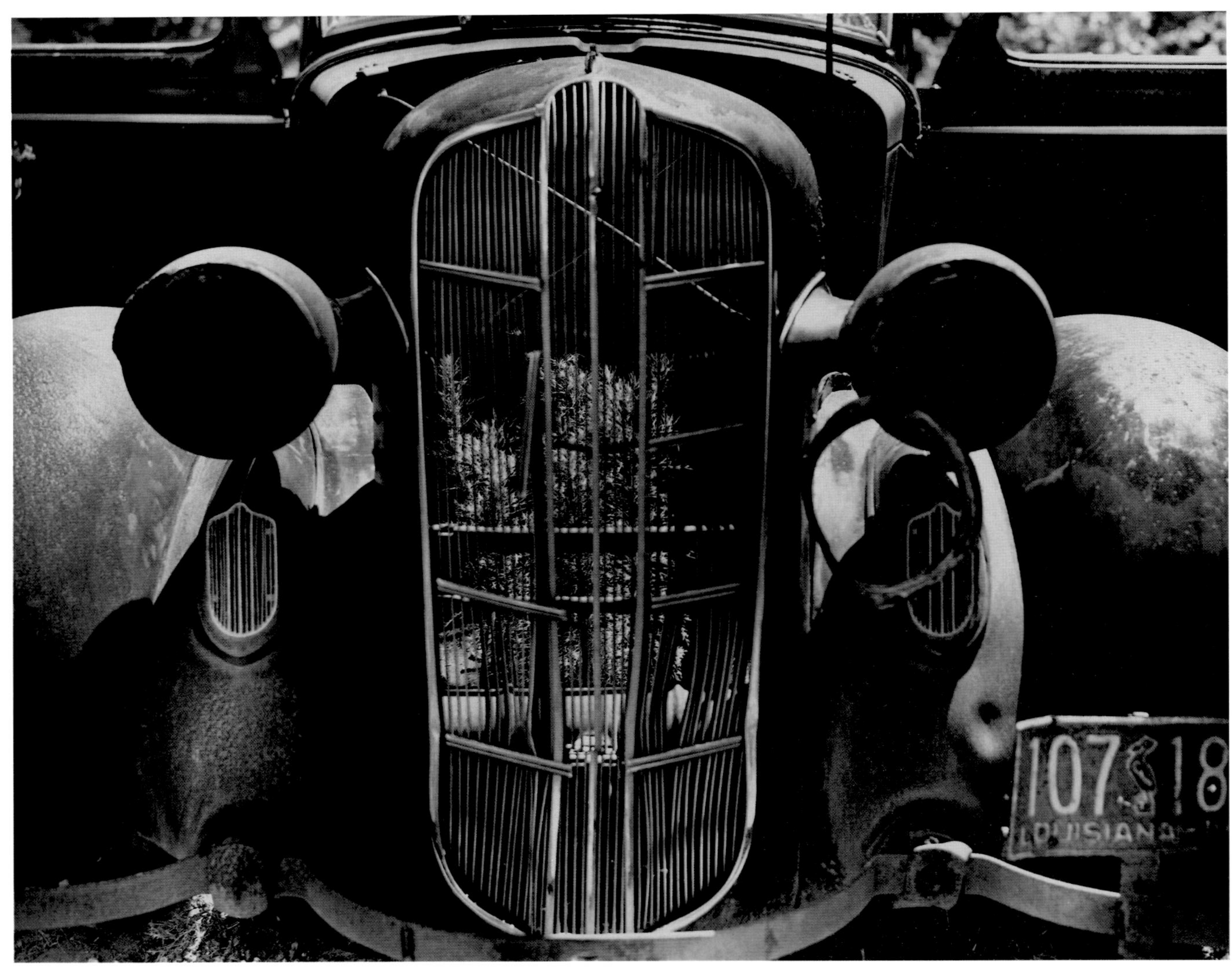

THE IMPRISONED LANDSCAPE

1954

"Some Observations on the Functions of Photography" (1939), typescript for a lecture

In the most "commonplace" objects marvelous new realities lie hidden, ordinarily unperceived relationships of forms, new combinations or psychological connotations, new aggregates of symbolic meaning.

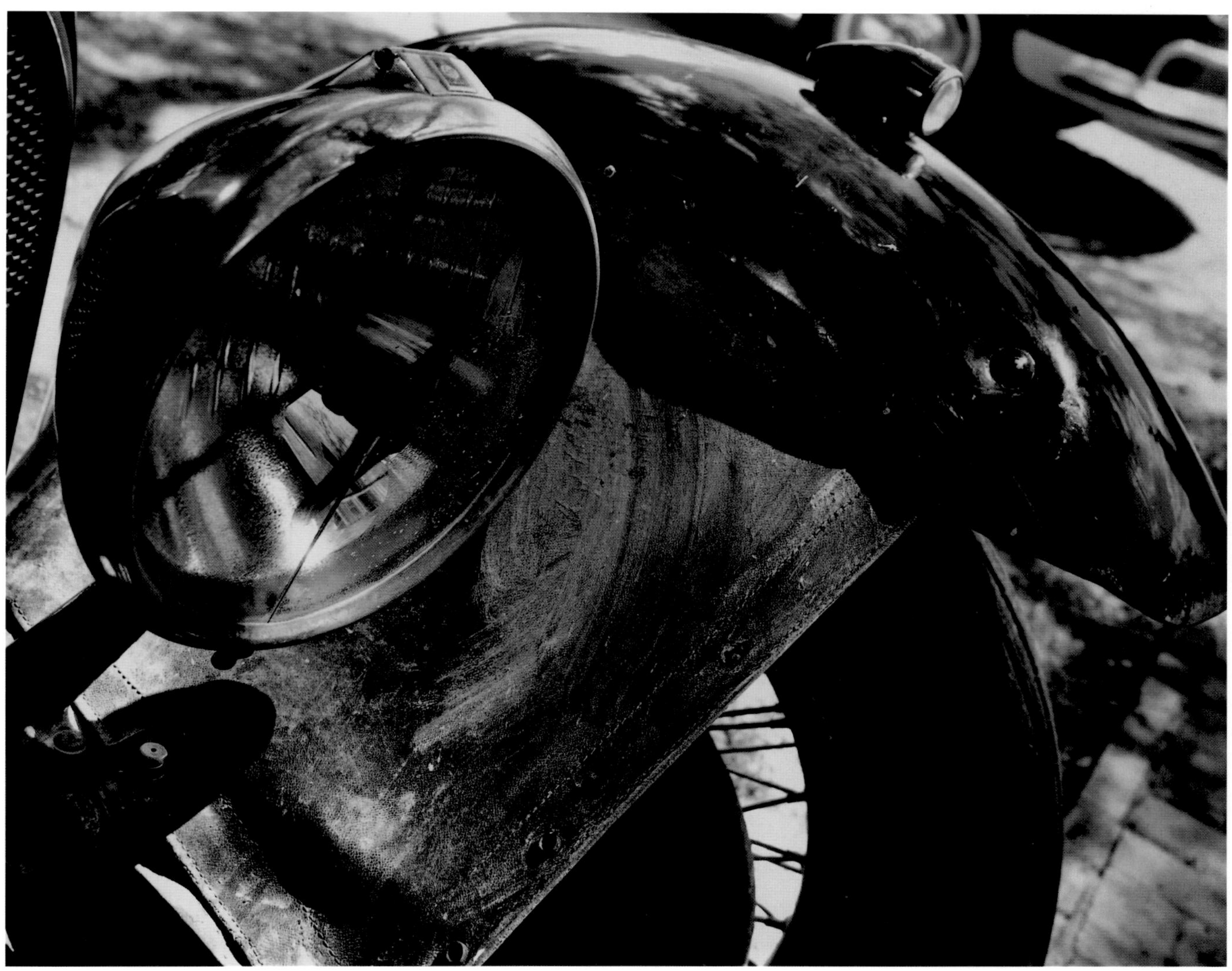

THE LEAPING SHARK

1961

André Breton to Clarence John Laughlin, July 31, 1942

I enjoyed your photographs in *New Directions,* and I am anxious to meet you. . . . The first issue of *VVV* has been issued; can we count on your participation in the October issue?

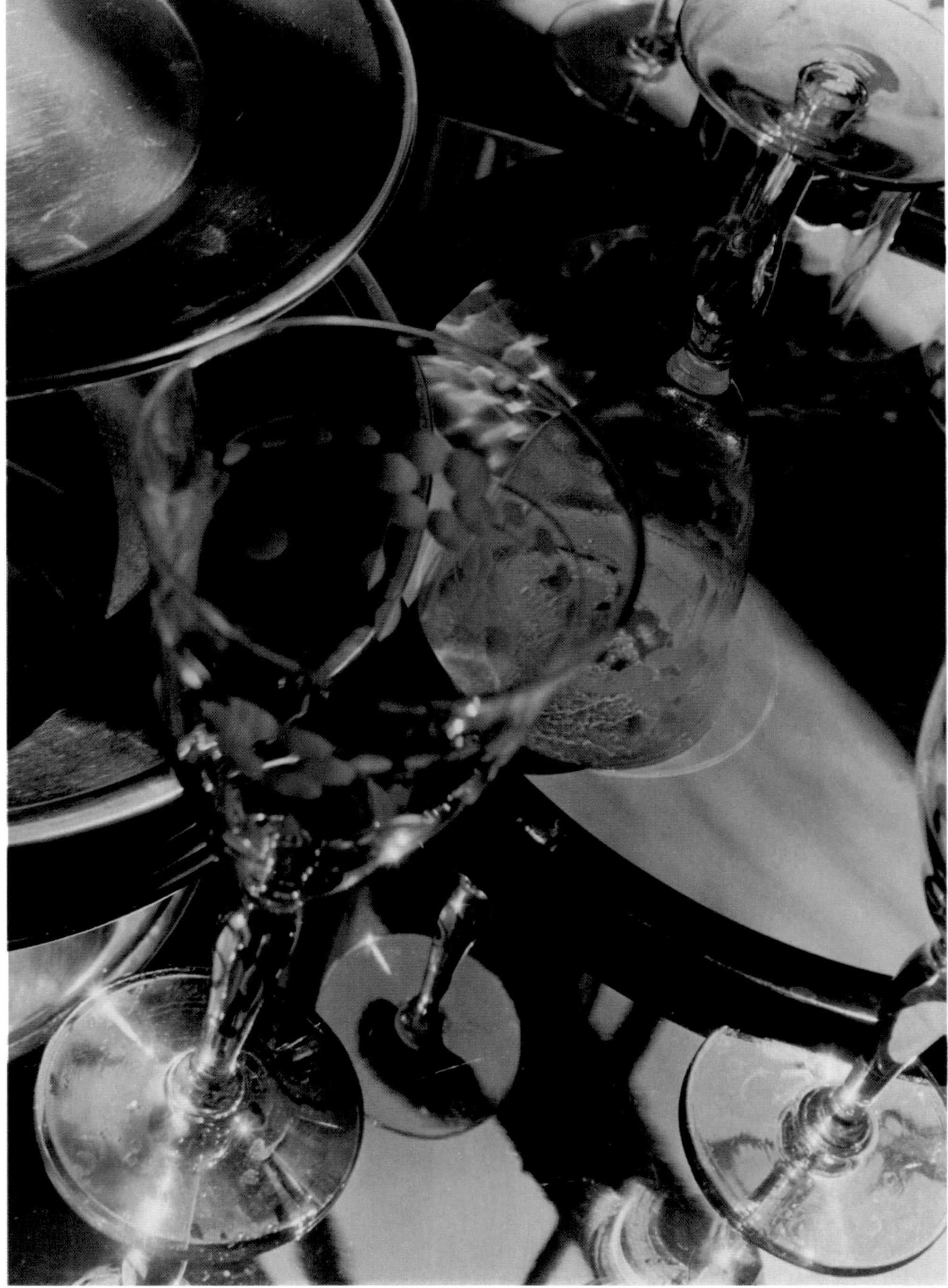

Opposite:
PHILODENDRON AND DOTTED SWISS
1936

Carlotta Corpron to Clarence John Laughlin, March 30, 1969

I have always admired the brilliant blacks and subtle middle tones of your photographs. The ones that appeal most to me are those where light adds life and beauty to the photograph. I like textures emphasized by sunlight, and also the fantastic and interesting shapes you are able to find in old trees, charred wood, etc.

DEPTH BEYOND DEPTH
1936

"Some Observations on the Functions of Photography" (1939), typescript for a lecture

I became concerned not only with the form and texture of the objects with which I dealt, but as well, and equally, with those objects which seemed to completely [embody] the dominant psychic states of the particular period which evolved them.

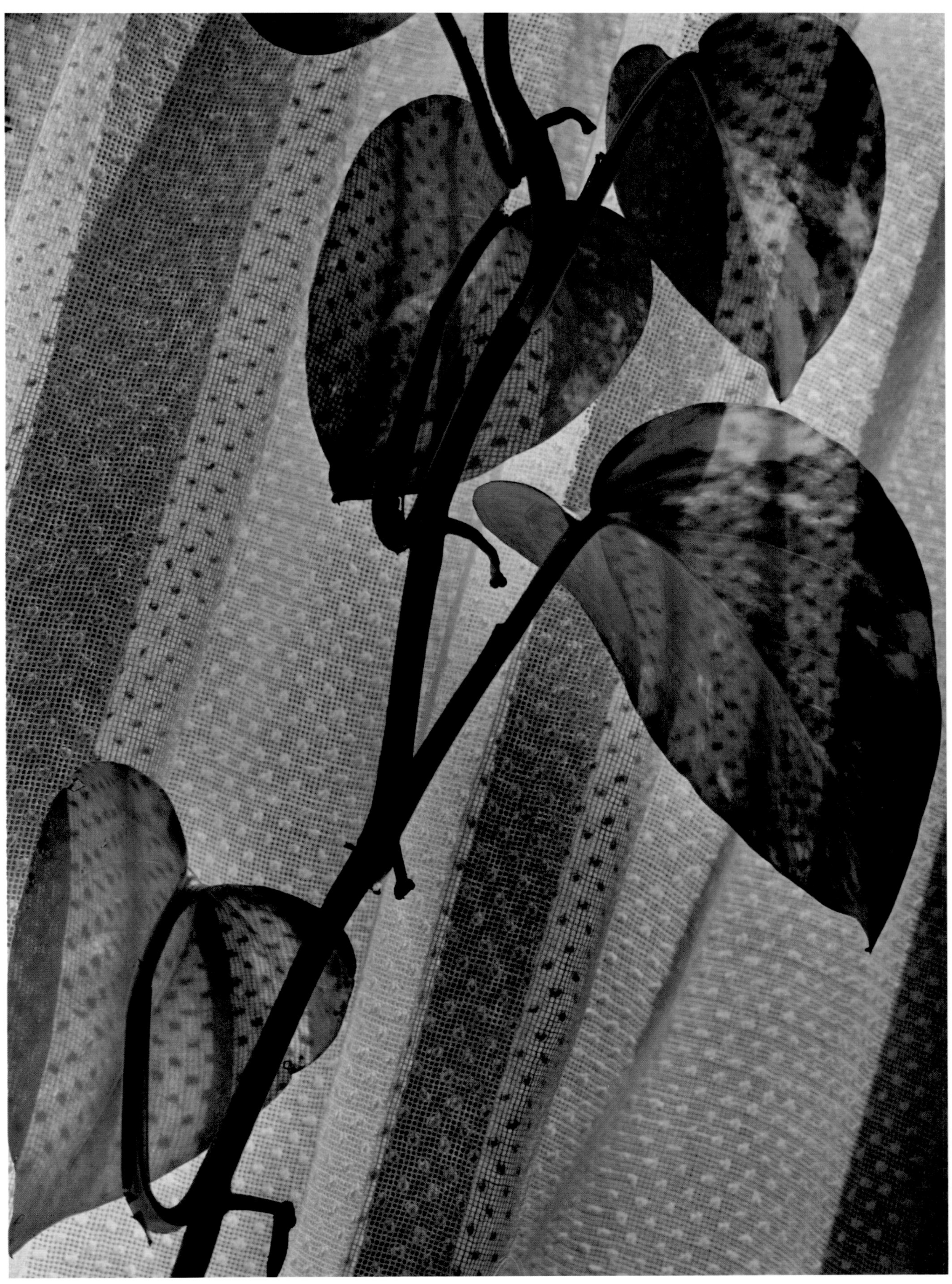

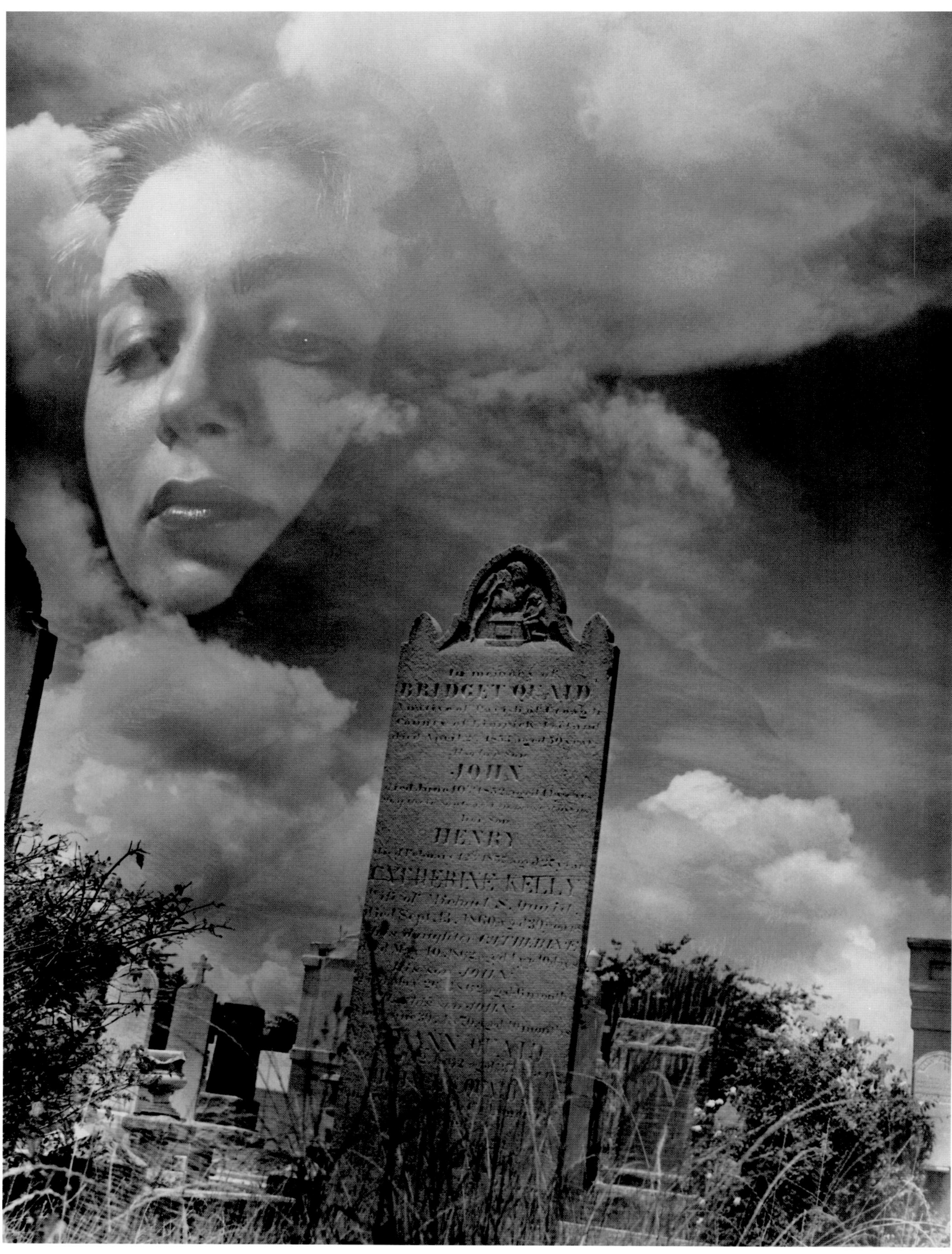
BRIDGET QUAID
JOHN
HENRY

Laughlin, Freud, Cholesterol, and Kilz: A Cajun Tour Guide Speaks of Peace

ALBERT BELISLE DAVIS

Good day to you, too. No, I don't mind stopping my work. Time to take a break from the brush anyway. Maybe make progress on my lunch while I'm at it.

You don't have to apologize for calling yourself a tourist. We're all tourists, aren't we? You can see that's true when you take a look at the booking sheets posted on these cemetery walls.

No, I'm not a painter, though I keep these canvas coveralls ready for October. Yes, I think that years ago these tombs were whitewashed, but latex paint is so cheap nowadays, and I've found a great primer that supposedly vanquishes mildew while it whitens. The primer's called — and this is a bit ironic — called *Kilz*. No, go ahead. I don't think having a good laugh in here is at all disrespectful.

This name? My aunt, great-aunt really. I try to clean up once a year. I can tell you for sure she liked a good laugh. No, I'm not what you'd call religious. I rather made a promise to my aunt before she died to take care of the outer walls before All Saints' Day. I know, I know. I'm cutting it close. I've got only a half day left of light. Then another deadline dawns. But I'll get the job finished now that the rains and mist are over and things have cleared.

Tradition? I guess it will serve me well someday to know I'm taking part in a tradition. Is it all in one of those books you're carrying? Let's have a look . . . *The Catholic Traditions in the Cemeteries of South Louisiana*. Yes, forgive me. You heard right to catch the tone of sarcasm in my voice. No, it's not because of the fumes. We're inclined in that direction in my family, a benign birth defect.

What's that other book? I know that one. Oh, yes, the photographs of Clarence John Laughlin. And you've marked . . . Cemeteries. All Souls' Day, St. Vincent de Paul Cemetery. Girod Street Cemetery. The black blurs of moving people, shadows everywhere. Done well, don't you think? Bringing up the old mortal realizations and reminders, right?

I like this one best. "Portrait of the Photographer as a Shadow." You

Opposite:
LOVE AGAINST THE FEVER
1940

Eugene Berman to Clarence John Laughlin, August 8, 1941

I like best the pictures in which the figures are not the central motive, but only part of the scenery, if at all.

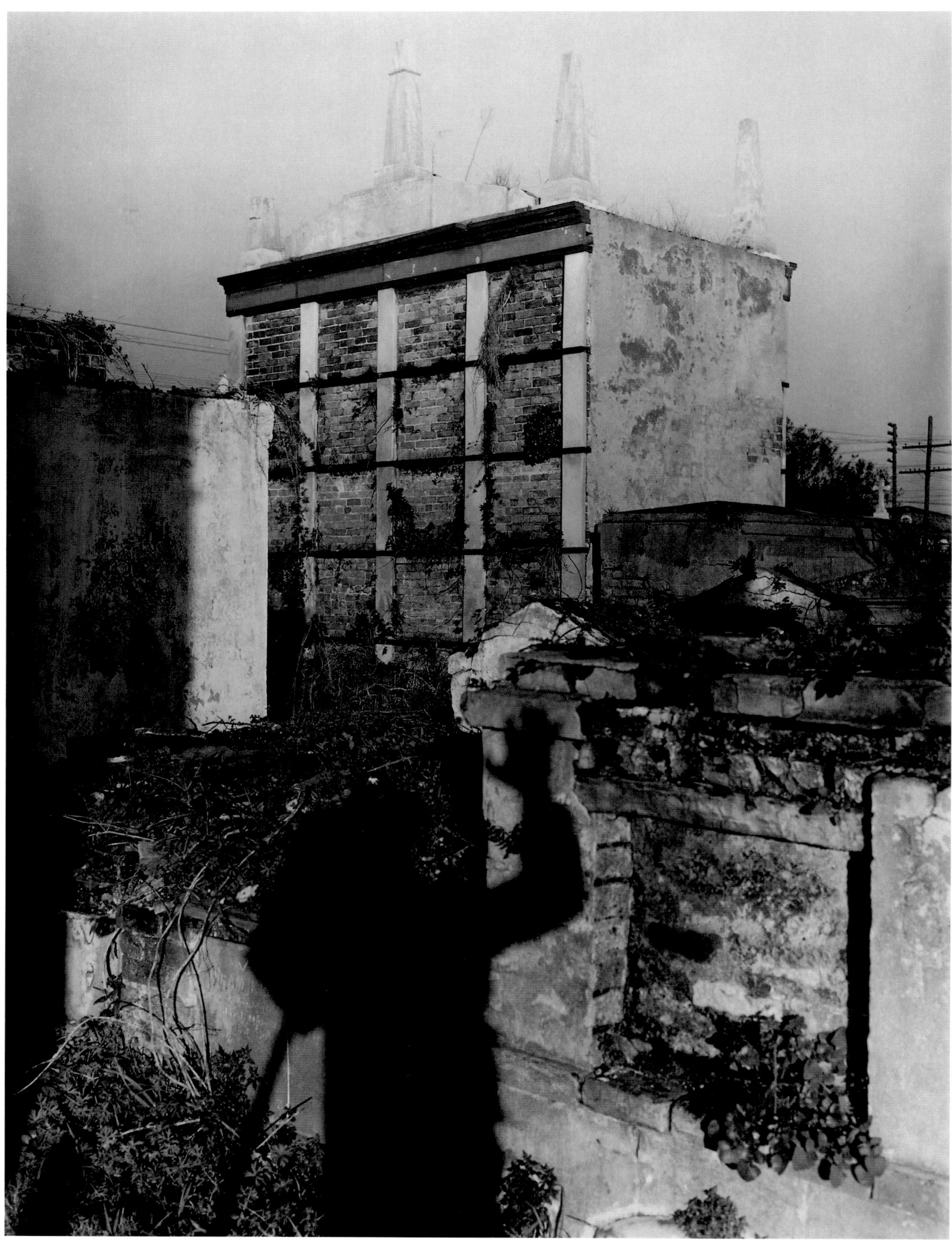

can see the photographer's shadow, his hand up as though he's touching the stone shafts. What's going on in this one, do you think? Yes, it could be just as solemn with the same realizations and reminders. Or did Laughlin find a kind of humor that day, just as we did today? And a bit playful, you know, mischievously playful and solemn at the same time, as he held his breath and lifted his hand. As though he recognized the irony, and he took a deep breath — thinking all the while maybe of the audacity that any mortal would dare paint on the walls of such an awesome city as this — held up his hand and held his breath to stifle the giggle. Forgive me, again. Breathing in these chemicals maybe has made me a bit knobby.

You went to New Orleans first, did you? How did you end up here, sixty miles south? Too *touristy* up there. I like that word.

But still, why travel all this way just . . . Ah, those realizations. Facing them squarely. Being at *peace* with them. *Peace*. I'm not sure I like that word as much as *touristy*.

I appear to be? *At peace?* Thank you, but I've never heard anyone label me that way before. And *relaxed* with it all? That's another word other people who know me would never use to describe me. Maybe it's the chemicals and coveralls.

But again, why travel . . . spend your time . . . Oh, I understand now. Heart attack. Close call? I haven't suffered like you, but I've thought about . . . Look here. Why do you think I'm having raw carrots and a banana for lunch? What was it Freud said about suffering? Never mind. Let's not get lofty with a carrot in the hand.

But, you know . . . Sit down there. Would you indulge me a minute or so longer? Maybe there is a kind of peace about me when I work in here, but you won't find my brand of peace in Laughlin's cemetery shots. I think I can tell you why.

Close your eyes a second. Close them. Do you smell it? Bread baking. There's an elementary school north of this cemetery. The wind's caught the cafeteria scent.

No, hold on. Keep them closed. What do you hear? Something else coming in from out there. Those children, yes, yelling, laughing, screaming, carrying on in the schoolyard sun. Quite a blaring little din they can make.

What do you feel on your face? Right, that same sun. It makes way from the outside, too.

Now open your eyes. See? Your hand goes to your forehead. Eyes tearing up? Such a glaring white. And look at the green of the grass, the blue of the sky in the cracks between the walls. I remember funerals in here and colors so intense every mourner had to wear sunglasses.

You see, on overcast days when you visit here, or seeing those tones of gray in the Laughlin photographs, you can't avoid certain thoughts. We leave this place with those realizations and reminders staining our cover-

Opposite:
PORTRAIT OF THE PHOTOGRAPHER AS A SHADOW
1941

"A Statement by the Photographer" (March 1955), typescript for Modern Photography, *not published*

In dealing with light, the photographer is dealing with one of the most fundamental, and mysterious, things in the universe. It is related, on the one hand, to the basic vital processes of all living things; on the other, to the inner nature of time. . . . We are creatures of the light, and photography is one of the most creative ways by which we can re-affirm this relationship.

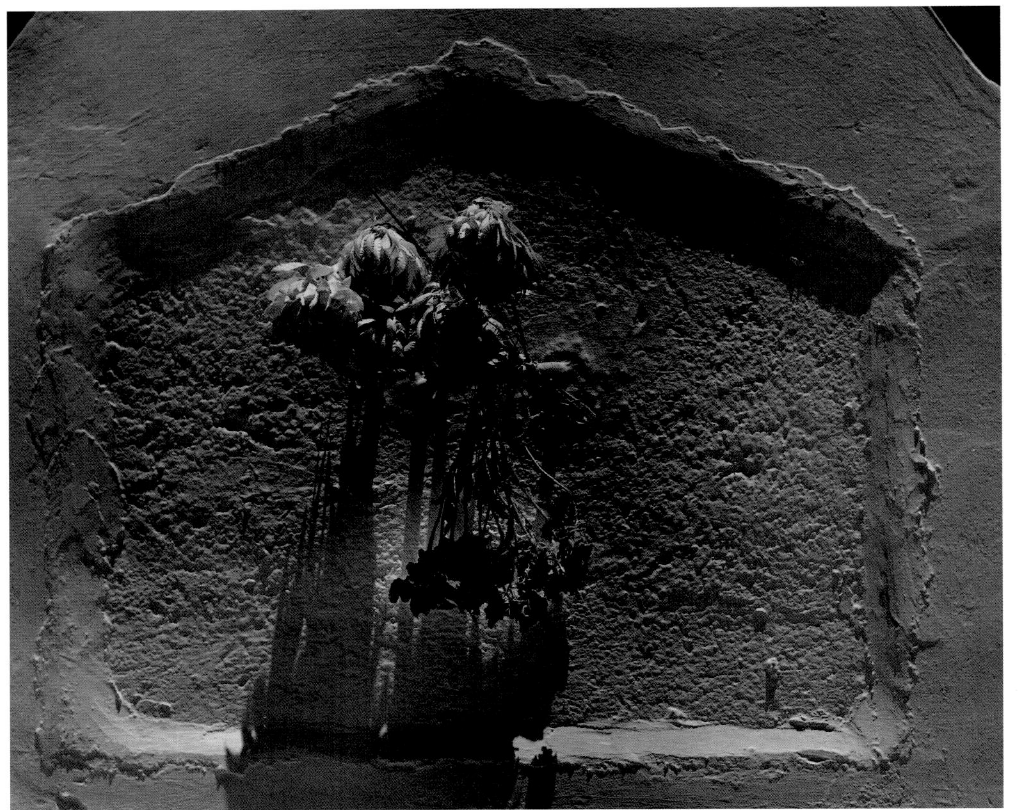

FLOWERS FLOATING IN THE LIGHT, NUMBER ONE
1954

Clarence John Laughlin to Hazel Guggenheim McKinley, July 10, 1941

Meanwhile, from the uncertainties of this age, this mad era of ours, we must turn perhaps, to the only certainties — the things upon which our senses seize, the things that delight our eyes, our ears, our skin and to the magic aura created about these things by memory — that so carefully and subtly magnifies the emotionally significant phases of experience, and suppresses all the rest.

alls. It's easy, isn't it, to believe sometimes that the shadows of this . . . this city . . . reach and fall beyond this city's boundaries onto the streets of that other city, that city out there with the bread and noise and sun? Easy to believe that the city out there was somehow built around this one.

Don't get me wrong, both cities call to us.

But on days like this — a day after a mild cool front has passed, a *coup de nord*, thin atmosphere, clear sky, full-hearted sun — you can understand that the truest impression is just the opposite of a gray-toned photograph. The truest photograph of this place would have to be in color, glaring blaring greens and blues, a white that makes you squint. A picture that reminds us that this city exists somewhere in the city of the living. My kind of peace comes from knowing that, for the greater part, in the contest of the two cities calling to us, it is the living city that somehow wins, with an effect so dazzling that mourners and painters and tourists have to wear sunglasses to walk among these walls.

Opposite:
THE NIGHTMARE TOMBS
1940

Patricia Leighten interview with the photographer, "Clarence John Laughlin: The Art and Thought of an American Surrealist," History of Photography *(April–June 1988), 144*

Everything, everything, no matter how commonplace and how ugly, has secret meanings. Everything.

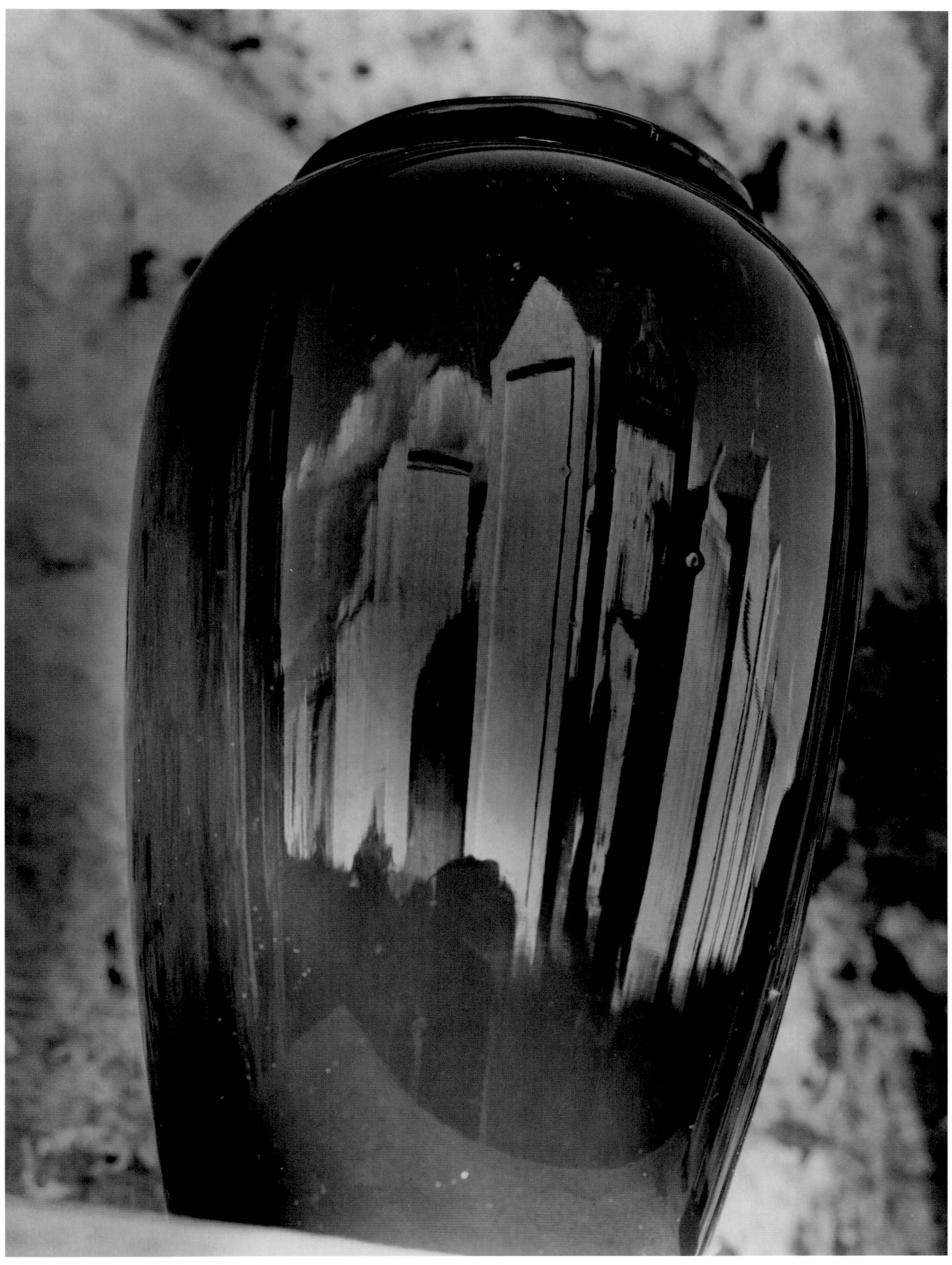

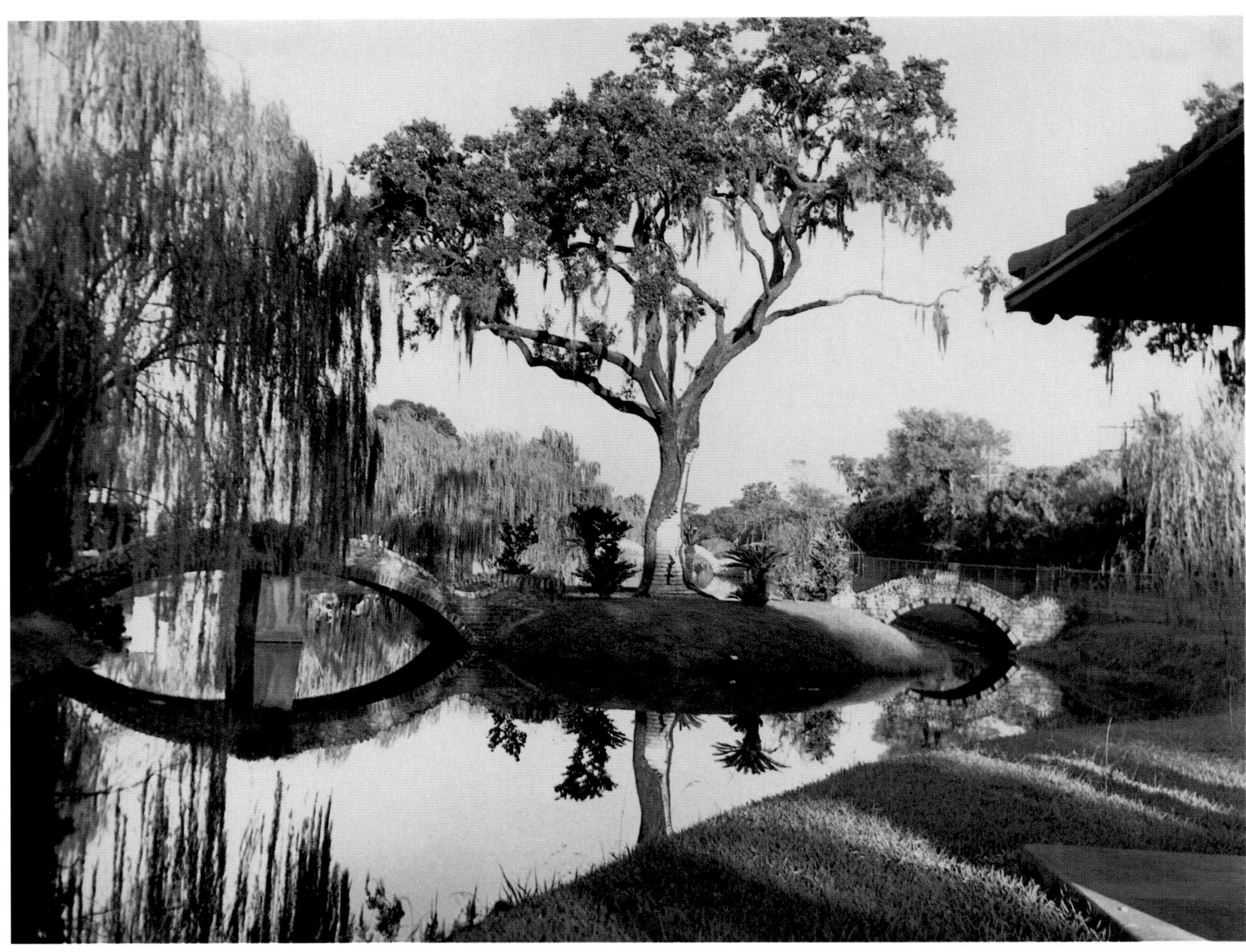

ENCHANTED LANDSCAPE

1938

Walter Conrad Arensberg to Clarence John Laughlin, June 8, 1949

I still prefer, as I was rash enough to say to you, an aspect of your work that you think less interesting than your surrealist effects.

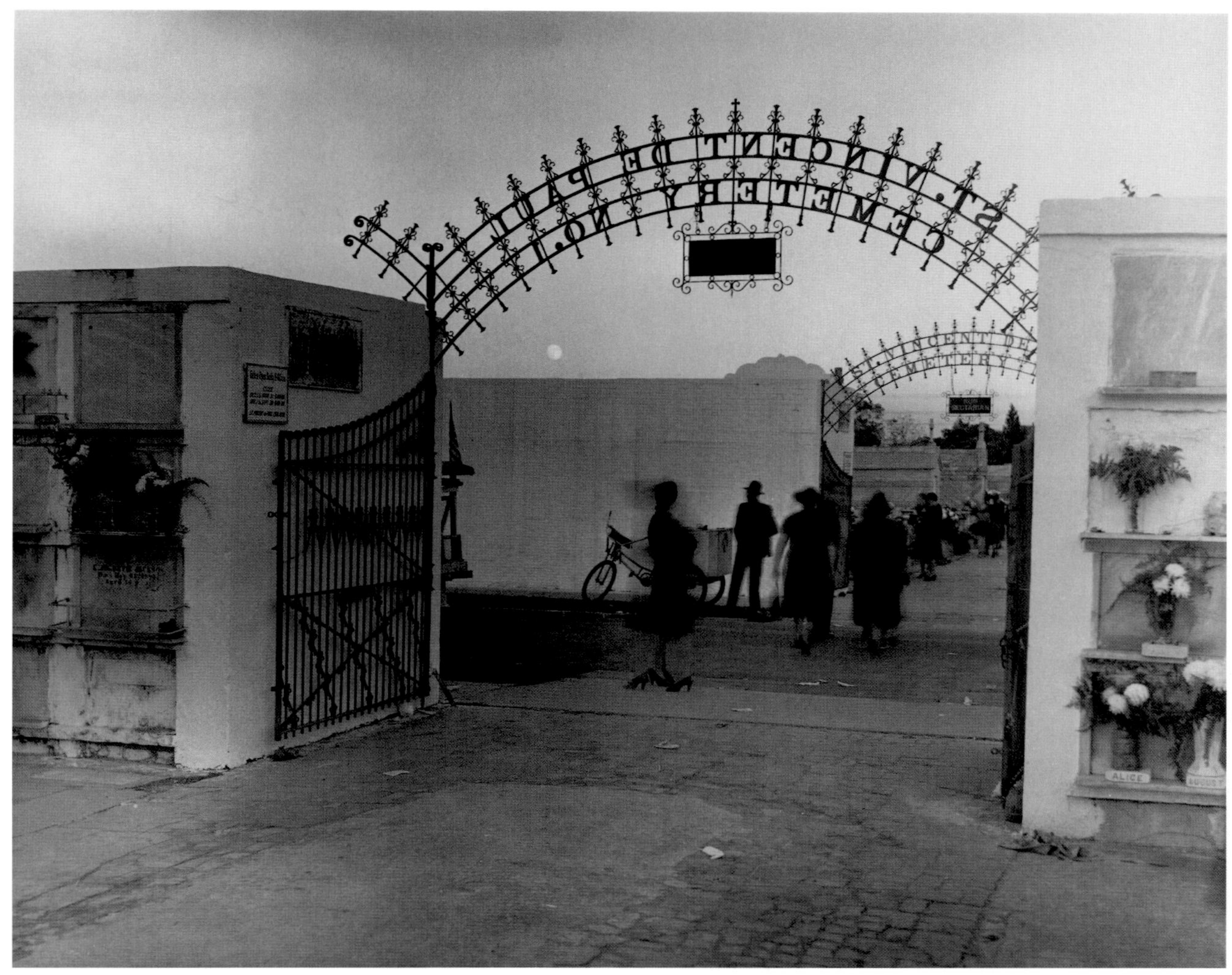

THE PHANTOM SHOES

1941

Clarence John Laughlin to the Dallas Morning News, *March 25, 1947*

I would, by far, rather see a technically "bad" but imaginatively "good" photograph, than one which is technically perfect yet imaginatively sterile.

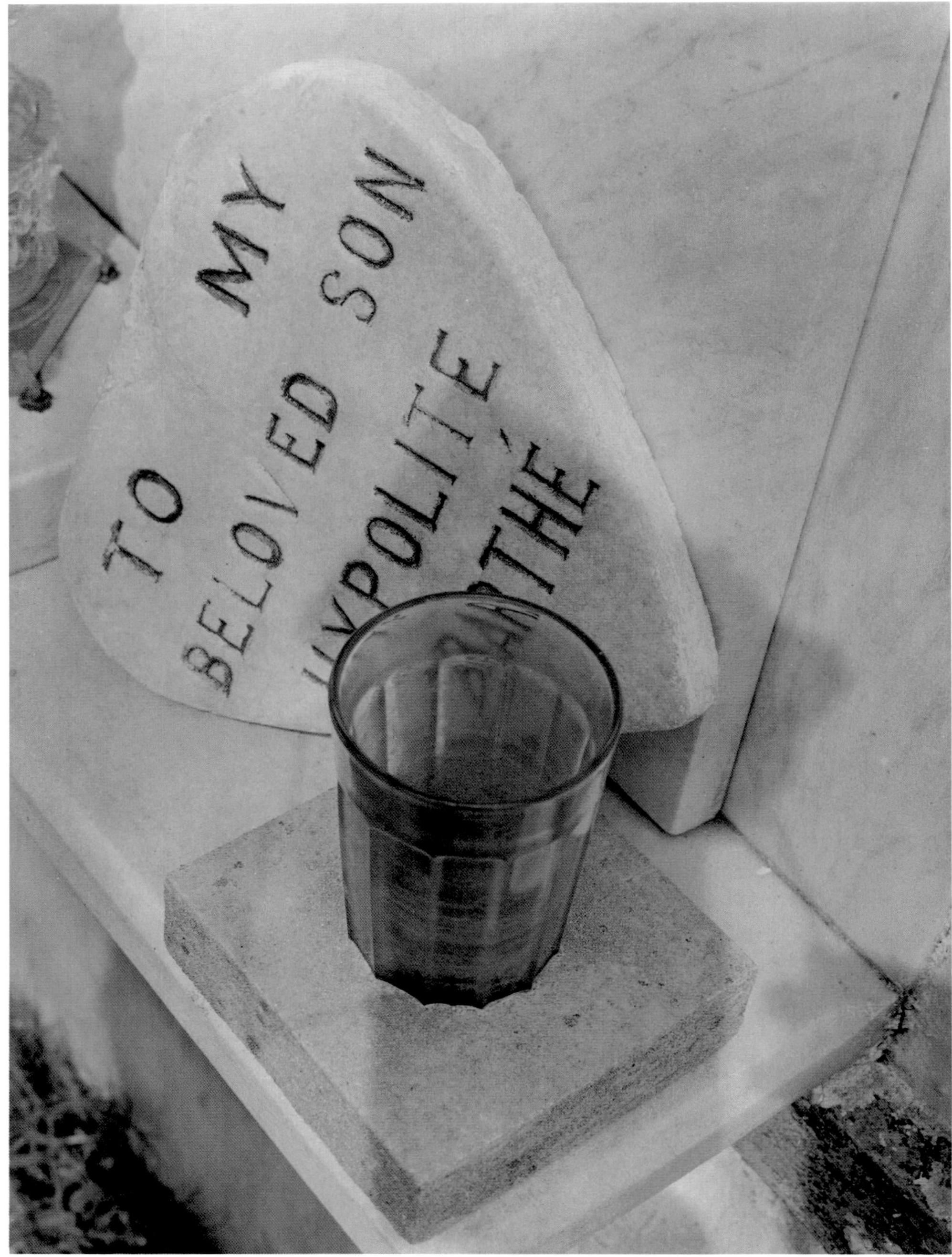

THE OVERTURNED HEART AND THE DIRTY GLASS

1937

"The Evolution of a Photographer" (1945), typescript

The first group, of course, was the "Still Lifes," and for a very definite reason. My feeling is that the beginner can find no better way of really studying composition. . . . In this group, as in all my work, there is a definite progression from the abstract to the poetic.

Opposite:

UNLIKE RECTANGLES

1937

William B. Wisdom to Maxwell E. Perkins, February 16, 1946

His photographs are crisp, clean-cut, sharp studies in light and shadow in which the composition frequently has a symbolic overtone or derivation. . . . Furthermore, unlike most photographers, he is educated and highly articulate.

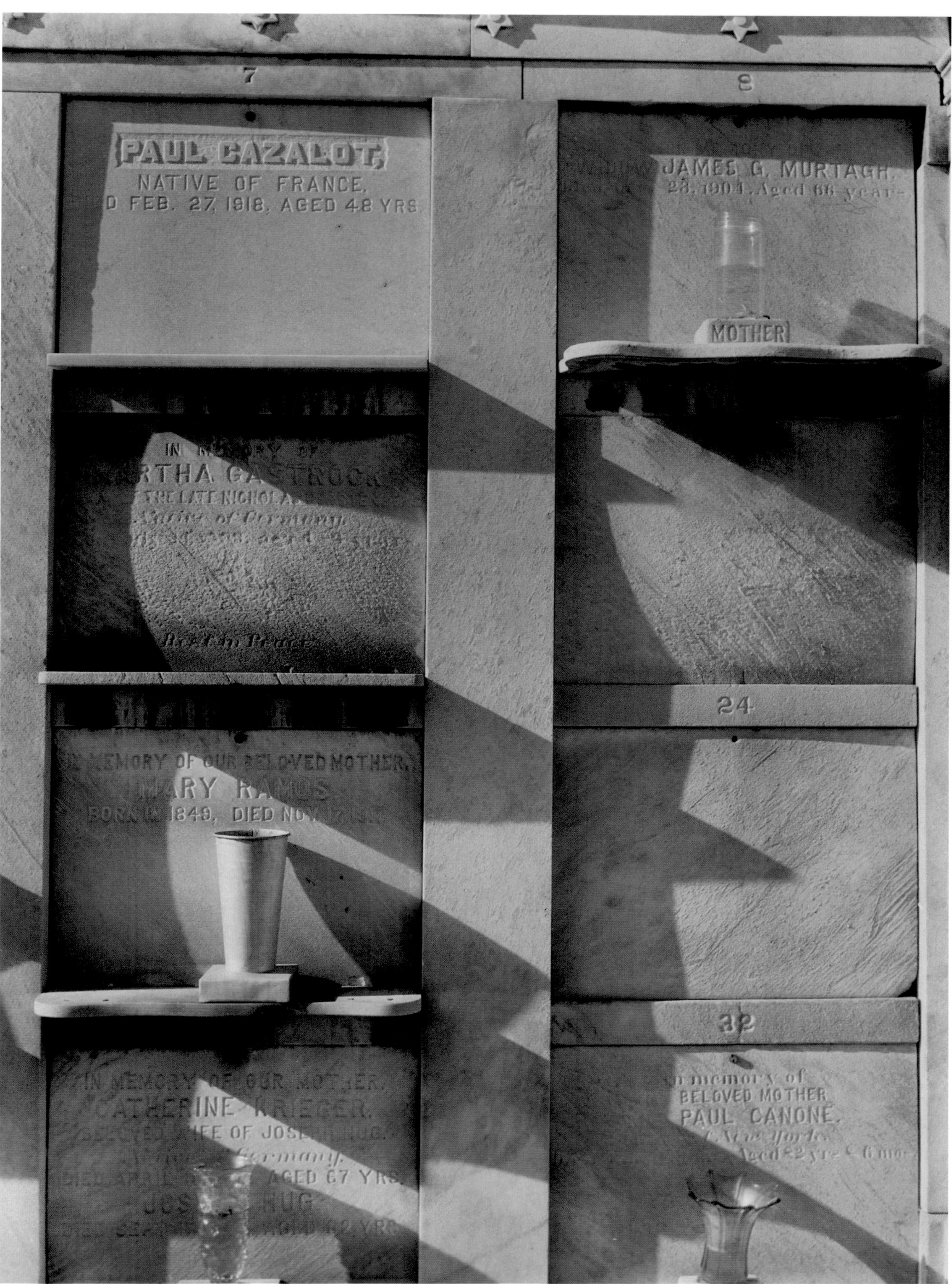
7
8
PAUL CAZALOT,
NATIVE OF FRANCE.
D FEB. 27, 1918, AGED 48 YRS.
JAMES G. MURTAGH
MOTHER
24
IN MEMORY OF OUR BELOVED MOTHER
MARY RAMOS
32
BELOVED MOTHER
PAUL CANONE.

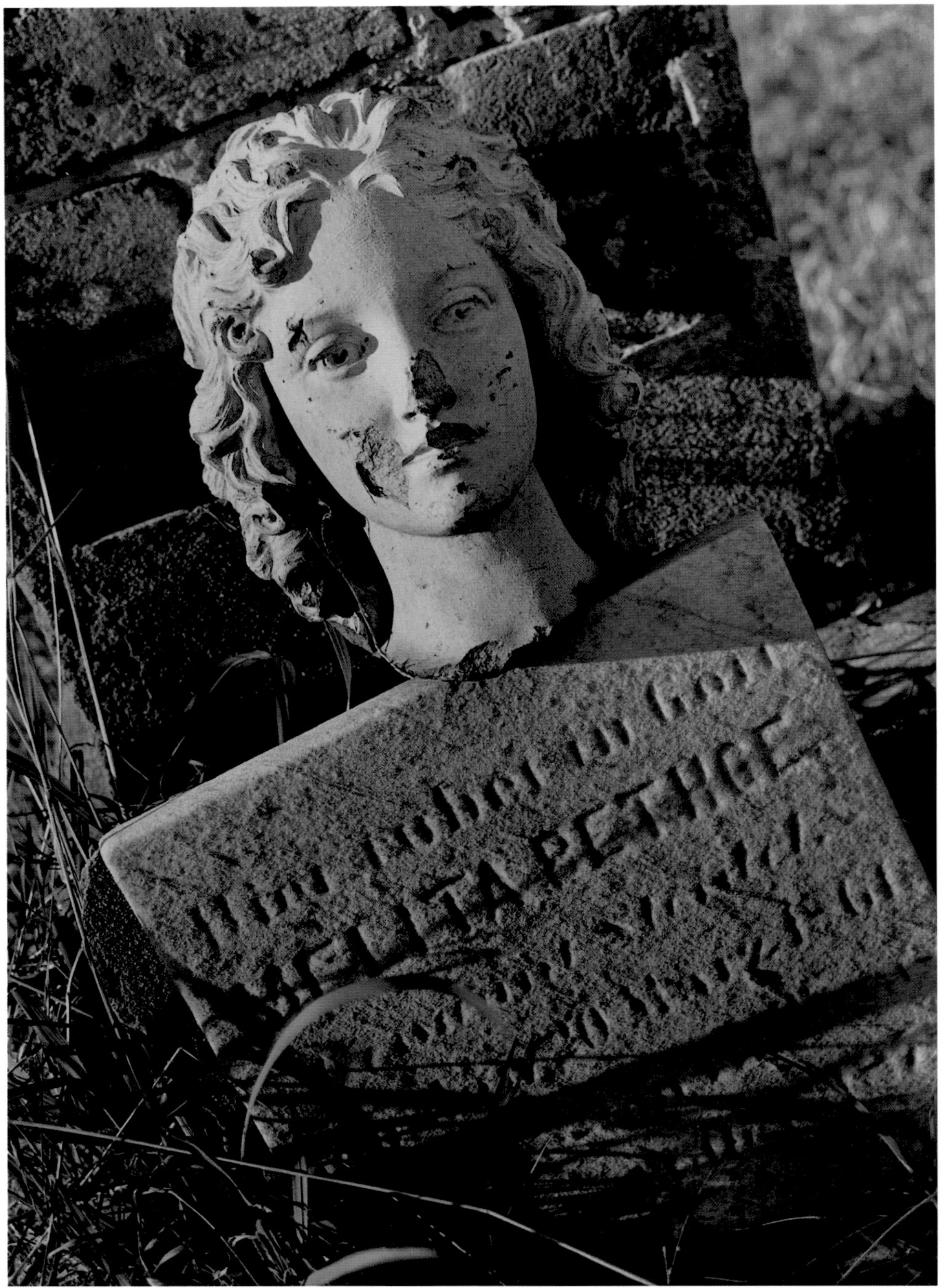

POEM AT SUNSET, NUMBER ONE

1939

"Poem at Sunset" (1939), typescript

I "saw" it in the profound sense of the word. The roots of that "seeing" are related, of course, to the very fiber of my being, the intricate web of interests and experiences that have built themselves around my consciousness during all the years of my life.

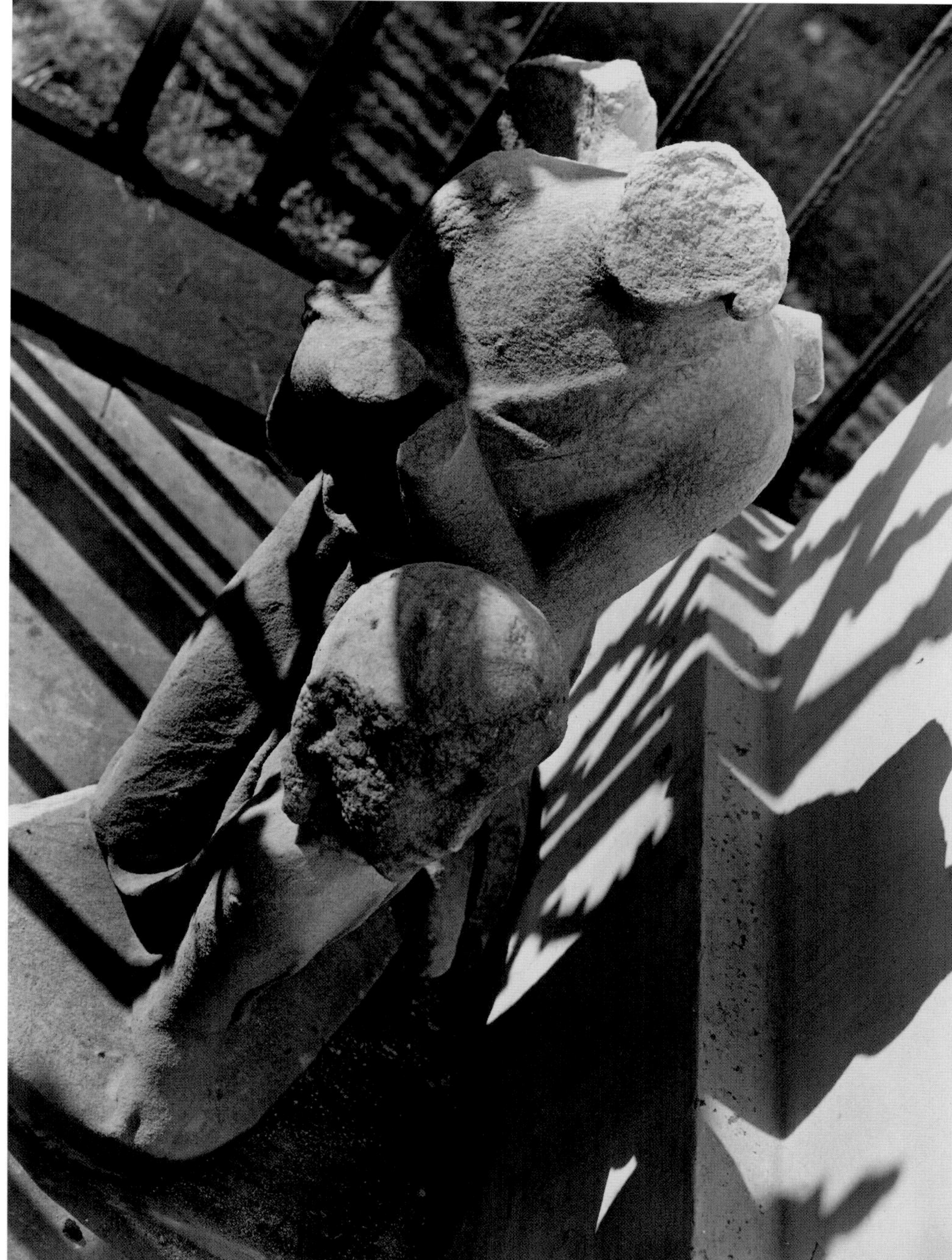

BEHEADED ANGEL
1939

Clarence John Laughlin to Julien Levy, April 26, 1938

I have a great deal more work, notably a long series of prints devoted to a number of extraordinary and unbelievable objects which I have discovered in the old cemeteries of New Orleans.

Opposite:
ANATOMICAL CASCADE
1940

Foreword to "Poems of the Interior World," Gallery Series Two *(Chicago, 1968), 34*

By a process of indirection, of imaginative transmutation, the most concrete object can become a symbol — even in a photograph.

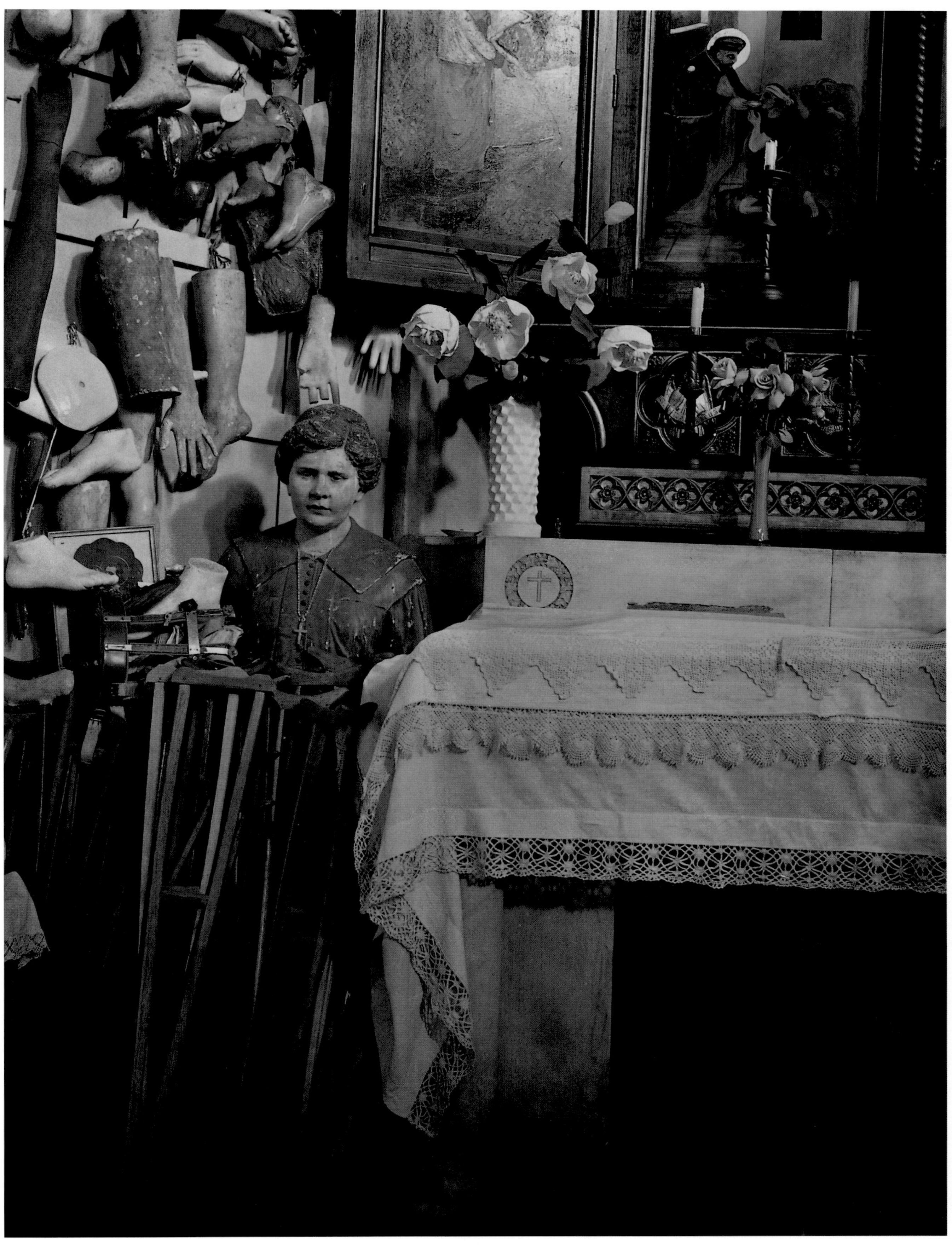

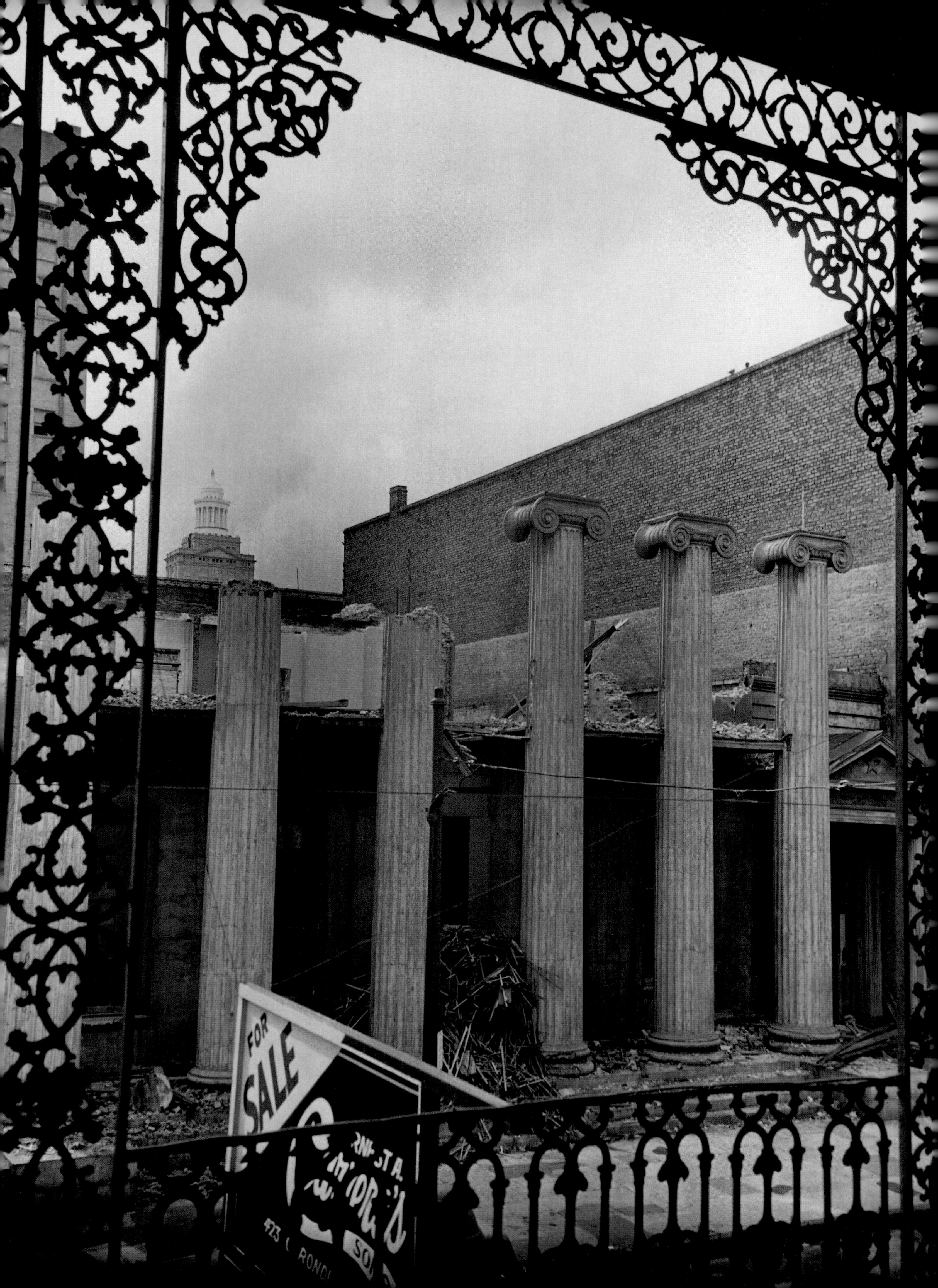
FOR
SALE

Terrible Beauty:
Clarence John Laughlin's Mythologies of Misery

JOHN WOOD

All changed, changed utterly:
A terrible beauty is born.

—William Butler Yeats, "Easter 1916"

Clarence John Laughlin viewed this century as darkly as Yeats viewed it—even Yeats at his most apocalyptic, Yeats at his most prophetic:

> Things fall apart; the centre cannot hold;
> Mere anarchy is loosed upon the world,
> The blood-dimmed tide is loosed, and everywhere
> The ceremony of innocence is drowned;
> The best lack all conviction, while the worst
> Are full of passionate intensity.[1]

Laughlin, like Yeats, and also like William Blake, another poet, artist, and apocalyptic visionary, constructed vast mythologies to give form to his thought and out of which he fashioned his art. He wrote that he "tried to create a mythology from our contemporary world," a mythology filled with "our fears and frustrations, our desires and dilemmas . . . so that the pictures became images of the psychological substructure of confusion, want, and fear . . . settings for the drama of the misery and madness of our time."[2] Most photographers are primarily interested in, to put it simply, making good pictures—which Laughlin did very well—but his primary concern was not the photographs but, like some Old Testament seer, prophecy and lamentation. Photography was merely the vehicle, the shape of his voice, the solidifications of his eye. "I am not primarily interested in the camera as a recording mechanism, but rather, in its possibilities as an extension of the inner eye," he once wrote.[3]

Laughlin's work is often called surreal because of his ghostly double

Opposite:
THE END OF AN ERA
1938

Typescript by Weeks Hall for U.S. Camera *(1941), not published*

His city wears an air, confirmed and expressed by its Carnival, of fantasy sobered always by thoughts of mortality. His New Orleans is also the Paris of Meryon, the Bermuda of "The Tempest," and the Brussels of Ensor.

exposures, as in "The Besieging Wilderness, Number Two," or his signature use of those shadowy figures of desire and fear that haunt his photographs of the graves and ruined plantations of Louisiana. But in a work like "The Diagonals of Peace, Number Two," which is radically different from what is usually thought of as a typical Laughlin image, we immediately feel something of Charles Sheeler and the precisionist aesthetic — or perhaps even Walker Evans and social realism, yet the modernist angularity and point of view of "Vieux Carré Abstraction, Number One," which is equally different from both preceding images, remind us of a Moholy-Nagy or a Rodchenko. And still other of his images are highly suggestive of John Heartfield's politically charged photomontages. And one could go on and on noting exciting parallels, but the photohistorians' and critics' inability to categorize and pigeonhole Laughlin has again and again led to his being excluded from the history books, neglected or even dismissed as a kind of unsophisticated and curious crank, just as Blake was dismissed in his time for some of the same reasons.

But Laughlin's stylistic versatility derived not from any lack of sophistication but from his willing use of all the -isms of modern art as mere vehicles in the service of his one overarching theme: the misery and madness of our time. And out of that misery and madness, Laughlin — like Yeats, like Blake, and like even Goya in his last work — constructed what might best be called "a terrible beauty." Our eyes return again and again to such work, moved by its beauty but also compelled by its ferocity.

Even in Laughlin's most placid images one always feels the hint of something disturbing, the certainty that something is going wrong. In those beautiful and seemingly peaceful images, a great deal has often gone wrong, in fact. The passing away and destruction of much of New Orleans and of so many of Louisiana's plantations served as Laughlin's metaphor for the ruin of the world. Of the twenty-three major thematic groups he arranged his work into, *Lost New Orleans* probably better typifies that sense of a terrible beauty than even those groups haunted by monsters, specters, and the furniture of our darkest dreams.

In his first book, *New Orleans and Its Living Past*, Laughlin described a photograph as so: "This once beautiful building exists no more. It has been destroyed by something more cruel and stupid than war — commercial vandalism. Where this structure once stood there is now a parking lot: typical of a here-today-and-gone-tomorrow civilization."[4] The specter haunting many of these images is no ghost, no patina, nor even the crumbling plaster; it's the bulldozer! And when it isn't the bulldozer that's ravaging beauty, it's neglect, as in the case of the plantations. And neglect surely is as much a by-product of the best lacking all conviction, as commercial vandalism is of the worst being full of passionate intensity. The passionate intensity of the *developers* — that flattering term the *wreckers* invented for themselves — to turn the world into a parking lot is no worse than the gut-

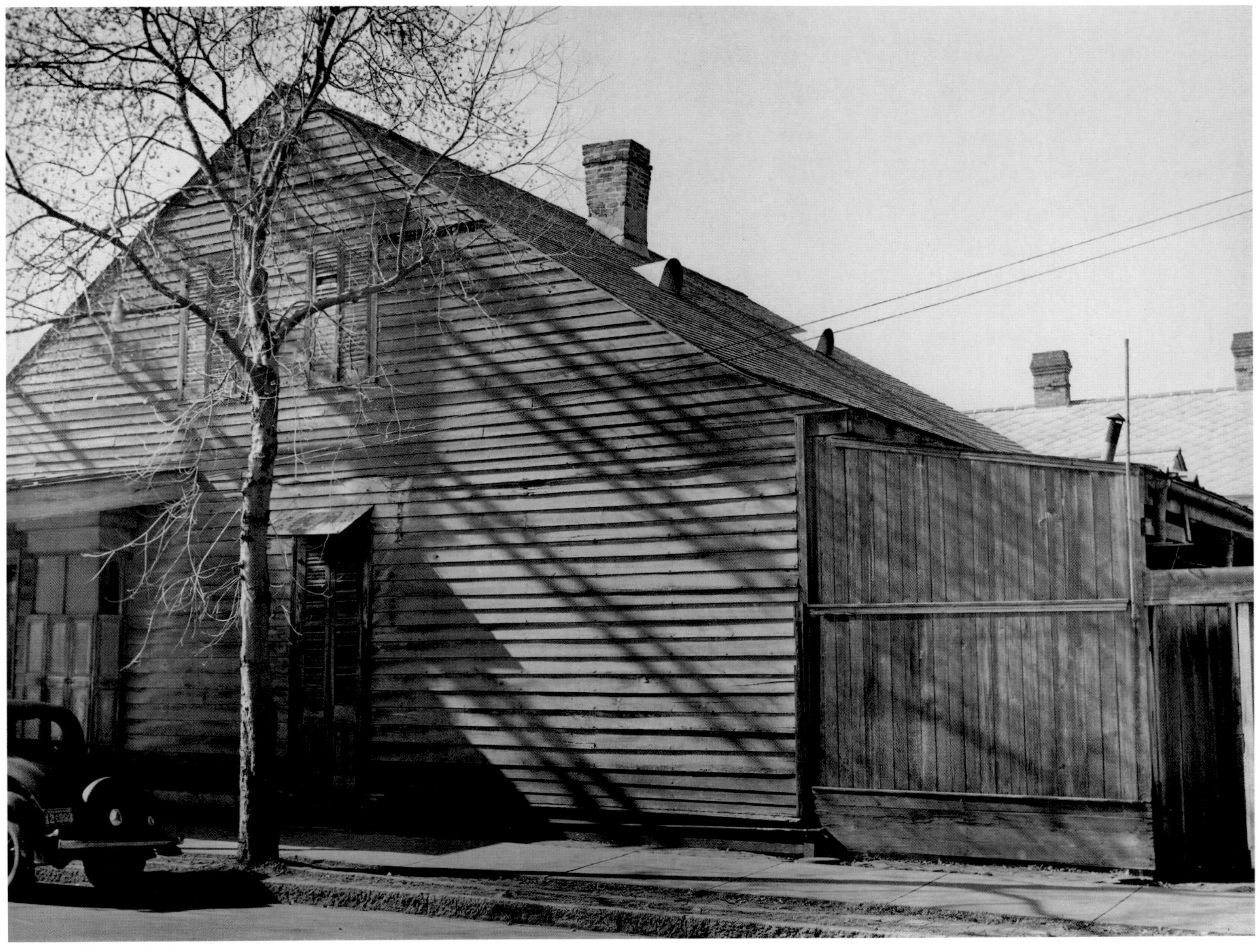

THE DIAGONALS OF PEACE, NUMBER TWO

1939

Weeks Hall to Clarence John Laughlin, December 1, 1943

To show the people here what people are doing elsewhere is too easy, too convenient. That is what the trouble with the popular conception of your own chosen medium [is]. Because anybody can photograph anything, your photographs are merely photographs. As well class Vermeer with a house-painter because both cover surfaces.

lessness of those who silently watch the wreckage go on or of those who have mindlessly accepted the lie that wrecking the past is the price of progress.

Laughlin was not one to sit silently — any more than those Old Testament prophets were — as his world fell into neglect and decay. But he did more than merely compose his jeremiads and rail against the loss in his books. The "Lost New Orleans" photographs are an attempt to save as best he could the city he loved from *development*. "Yes, how different the Quarter was then from the Quarter of now! Because, like the old sections of Paris, it looked old and it *felt* old. It had *no* pretentions. It was not 'spruced up' or 'slicked up' to appear something other than what it was. It was *itself* — without apology, and without pretense."[5] Photography for Clarence John Laughlin was always poetry and prophecy, but finally it also became a sacred act of preservation.

Notes

1. "The Second Coming" from *Selected Poems and Two Plays of William Butler Yeats*, M. L. Rosenthal, ed. (New York: Collier Books, 1966), 91.
2. In *Clarence John Laughlin: The Transforming Eye* (New York: International Exhibitions Foundation and the Lunn Gallery/Graphics International, 1976), n.p.
3. Letter from Clarence John Laughlin to Stark Young, March 26, 1946, in the Clarence John Laughlin Papers, The Historic New Orleans Collection.
4. Clarence John Laughlin and David L. Cohn, *New Orleans and Its Living Past* (Boston: Houghton Mifflin, 1941), plate L.
5. Clarence John Laughlin, *Lost Louisiana*, unpublished manuscript, p. 60, in the Clarence John Laughlin Papers, The Historic New Orleans Collection.

MODULATED SHADOWS, NUMBER ONE
1940

Clarence John Laughlin to Margaret Bourke-White, 1936

I feel convinced that whole new worlds lie about us, sheathed in what we call the "commonplaceness" of reality.

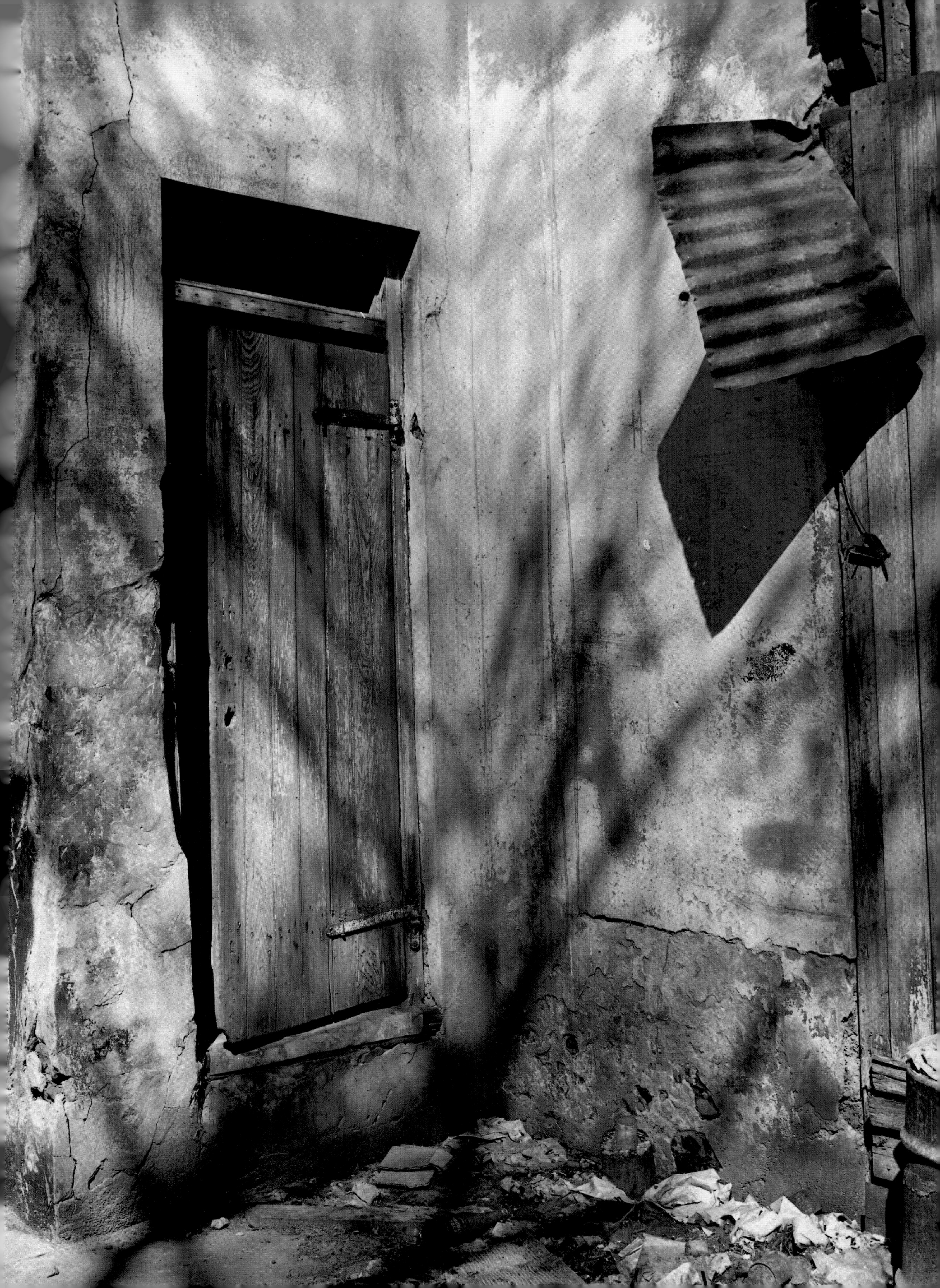

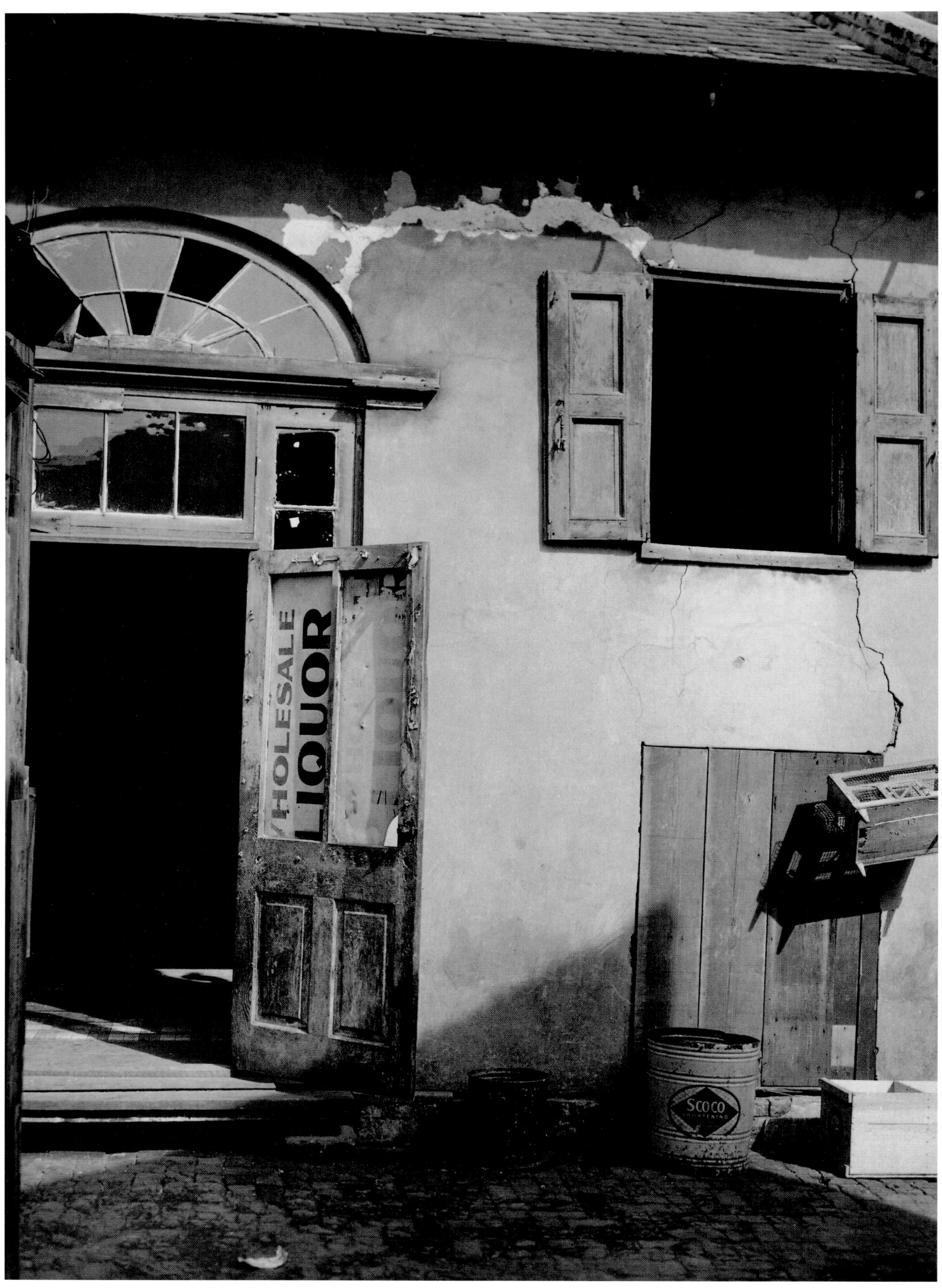
HOLESALE
LIQUOR
Scoco

Opposite:

A STRANGE SITUATION

1938

Clarence John Laughlin's caption

Another attempt to convey the special "feel" of the poorer sections of the Vieux Carré. The door is partly composed of old advertising signs, the box clings to the wall and seems to defy gravity; the window yawns and the white streak on the wall connects the window with the fan window.

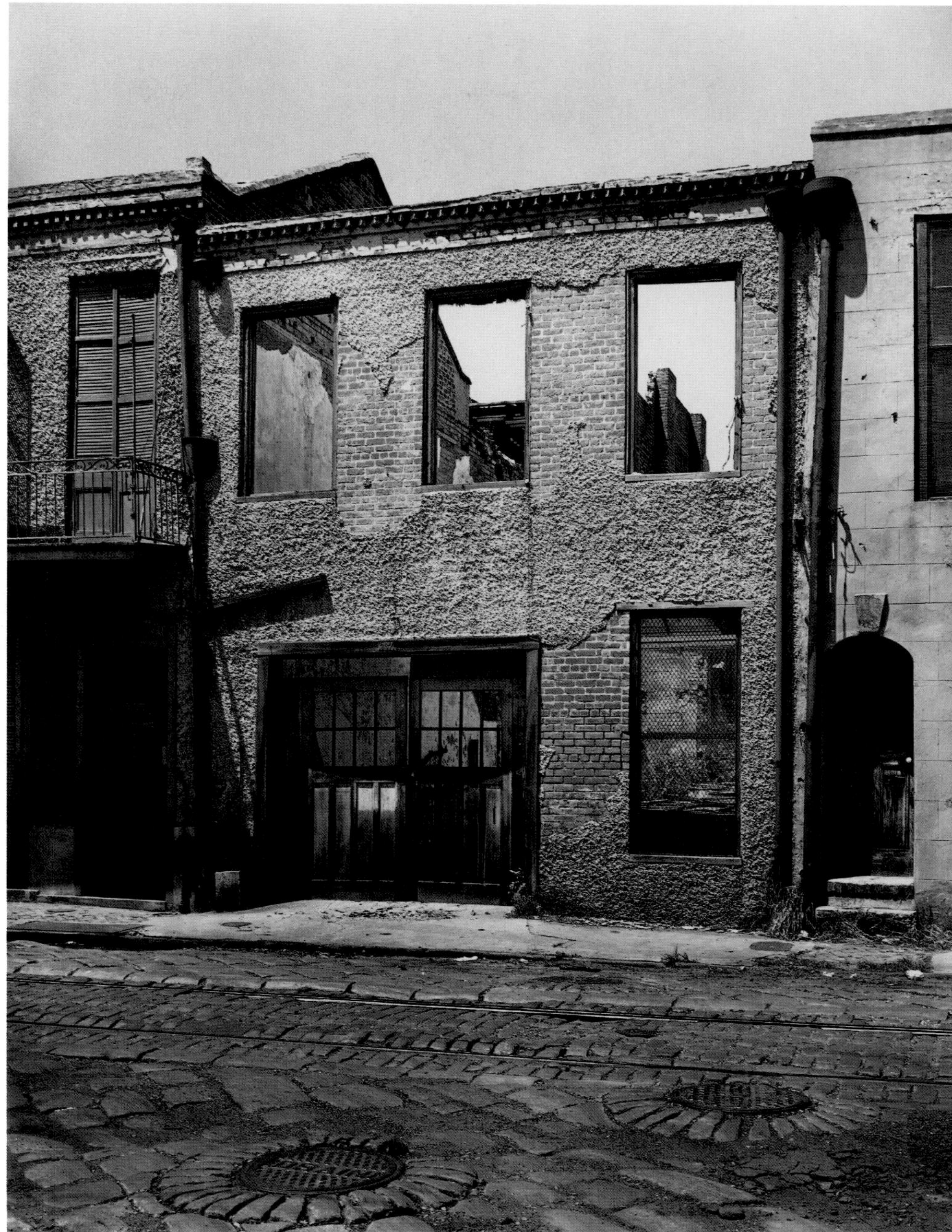

VISTAS IN A SHELL

1940

Robin Feild to Clarence John Laughlin, June 7, 1945

As you probably know, I hate [New Orleans] and think that perhaps its only justification is for its decay to be recorded in your photographs and then — the deluge of fire and brimstone as far as I'm concerned! I have never been able to see it in any historic perspective. It has always seemed to me to reflect the worst possible elements of a society which was in decay when it originally endeavored to claim some good earth out of the swamplands.

Opposite:
VIEUX CARRÉ ABSTRACTION, NUMBER ONE
1938

"Some Observations on the Functions of Photography" (1939), typescript for a lecture

I envisaged the central problem clearly: dealing with the vast complex totality of a city in which the present and past discordantly mingled.

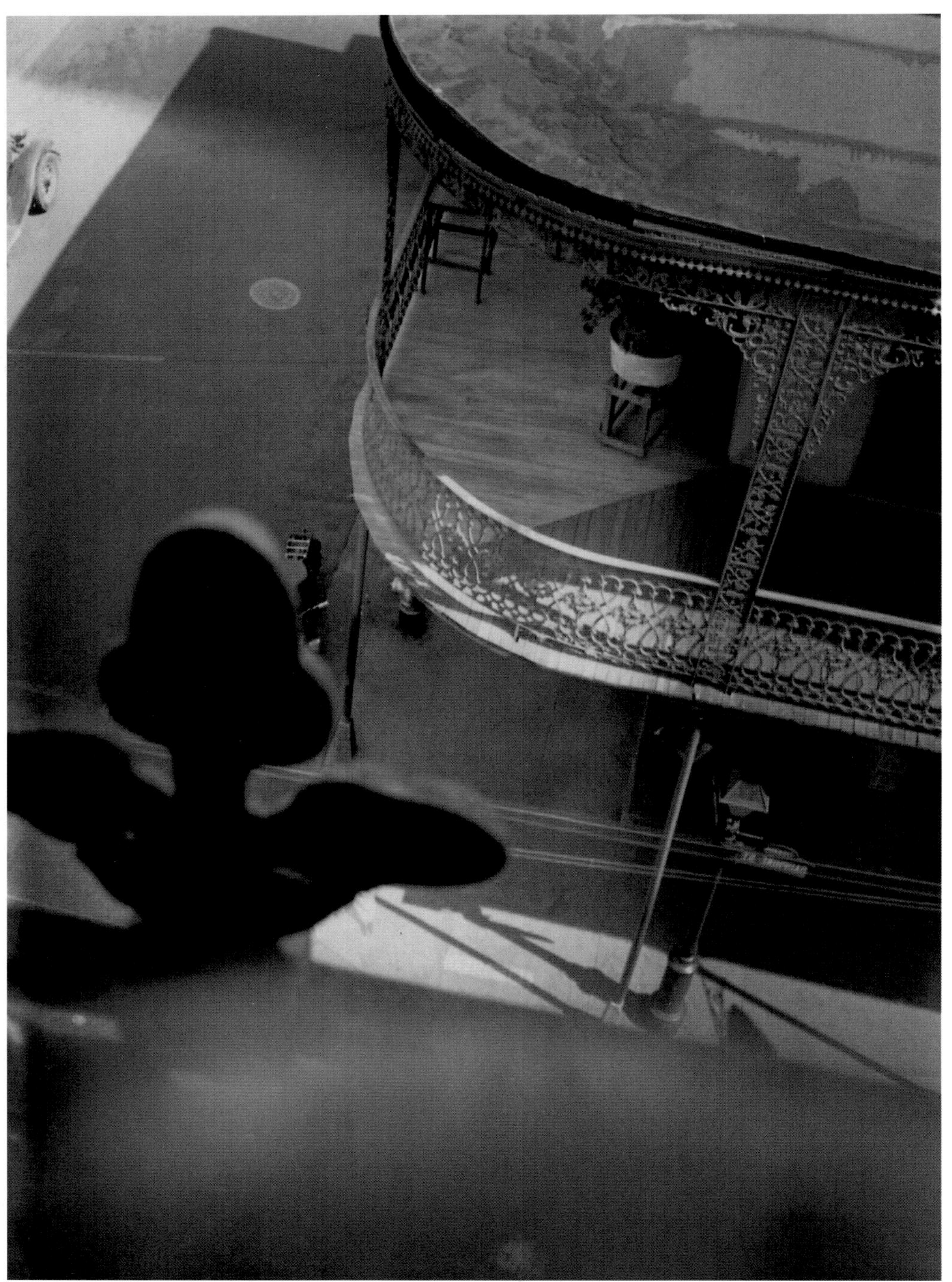

UNDER THE AEGIS OF THE ACORN
1935

Fritz Gruber, "Clarence John Laughlin: A Mystic of the Camera," Photo-Prisma *(February 1960), typescript translation by Dr. Eric Albrecht*

He is, in a sense, the Baudelaire of the camera. He discovers the secret, and the ambiguous revivifies what has for a long time been under dust, what has died, and vanished.

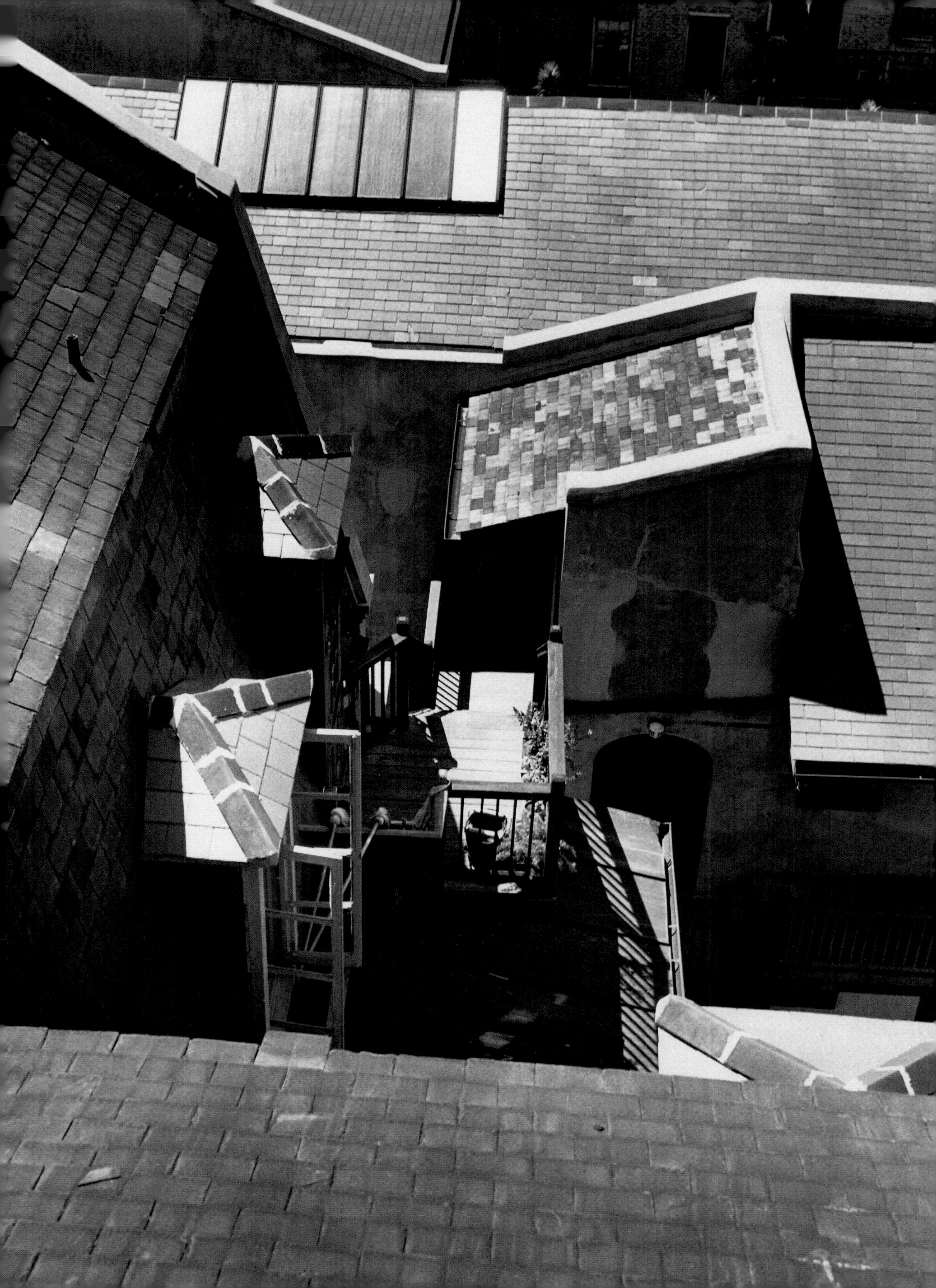

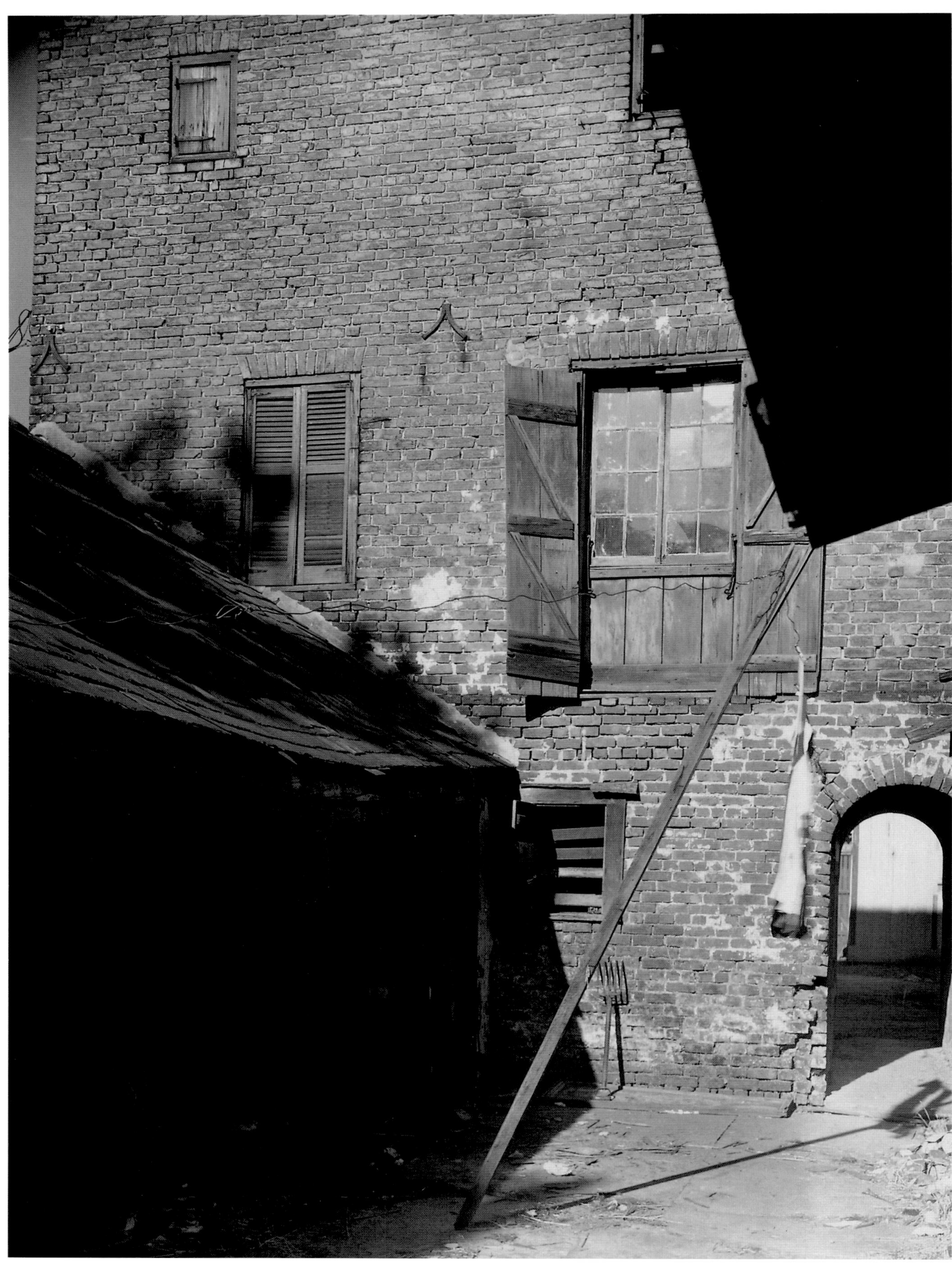

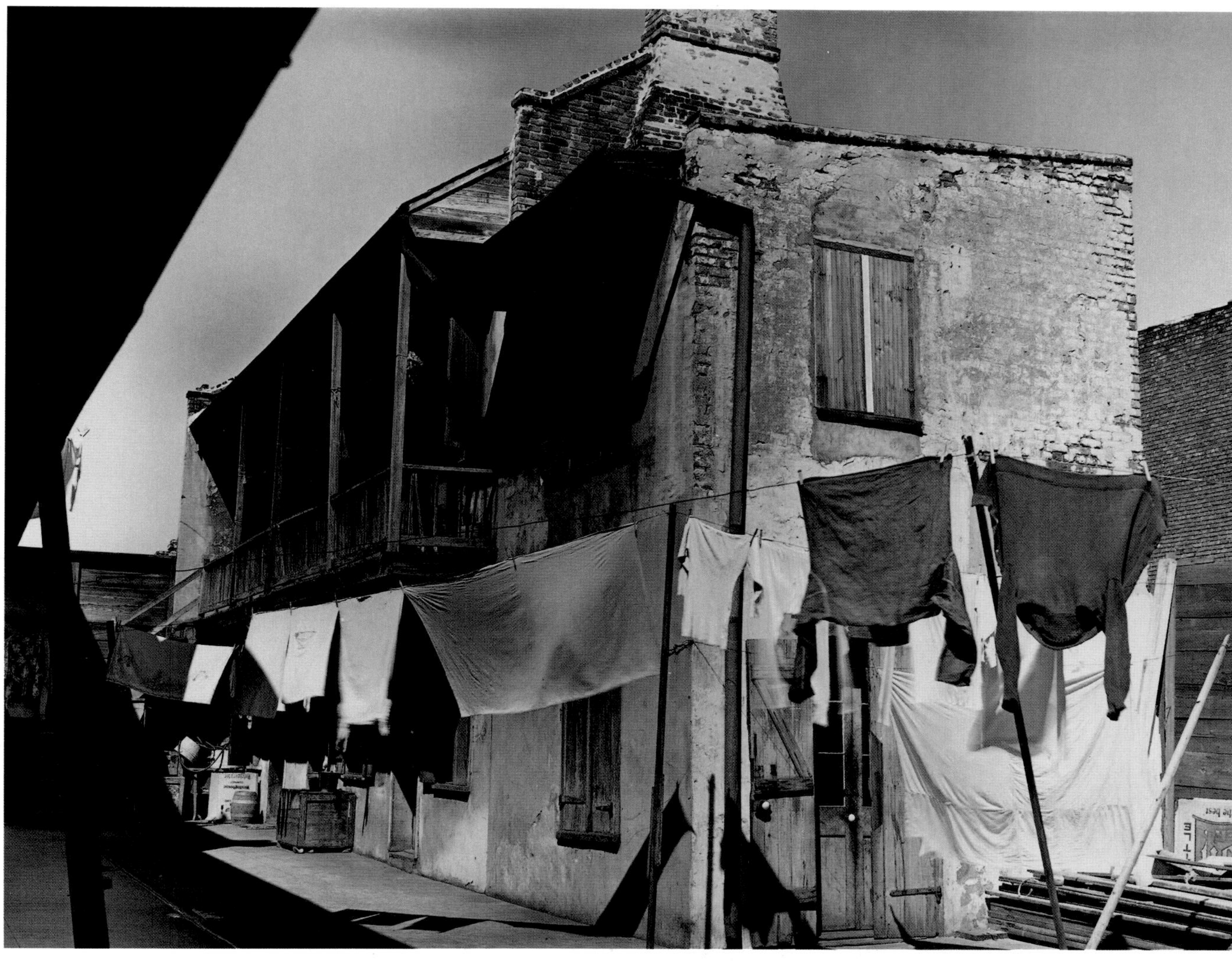

Opposite:
FROM AN EARLIER TIME, NUMBER EIGHT
1941

Lost Louisiana, *typescript of unpublished book, 60*

[The shadows] suggested a pervasive sense of mystery — of life hidden behind the outer surfaces. . . . For, indeed — night or day — most of the Quarter of that time had this subtle feeling of life fully and intensely lived, but hidden from view.

Above:
THE DAILY WASH
1940

Lost Louisiana, *typescript of unpublished book, 60*

Yes, how different the Quarter was then from the Quarter of now! Because, like the old sections of Paris, it looked old and it *felt* old. It had *no* pretensions. It was not "spruced up" or "slicked up" to appear something other than what it was. It was itself — without apology, and without pretense.

Overleaf:
THE BESIEGING WILDERNESS, NUMBER TWO
1938

Joseph Cornell to Clarence John Laughlin, January 13, 1948

Nor have I forgotten the initial pleasure of seeing your work at ART OF THIS CENTURY evoking all kinds of wonderful things about what I dreamed about the South.

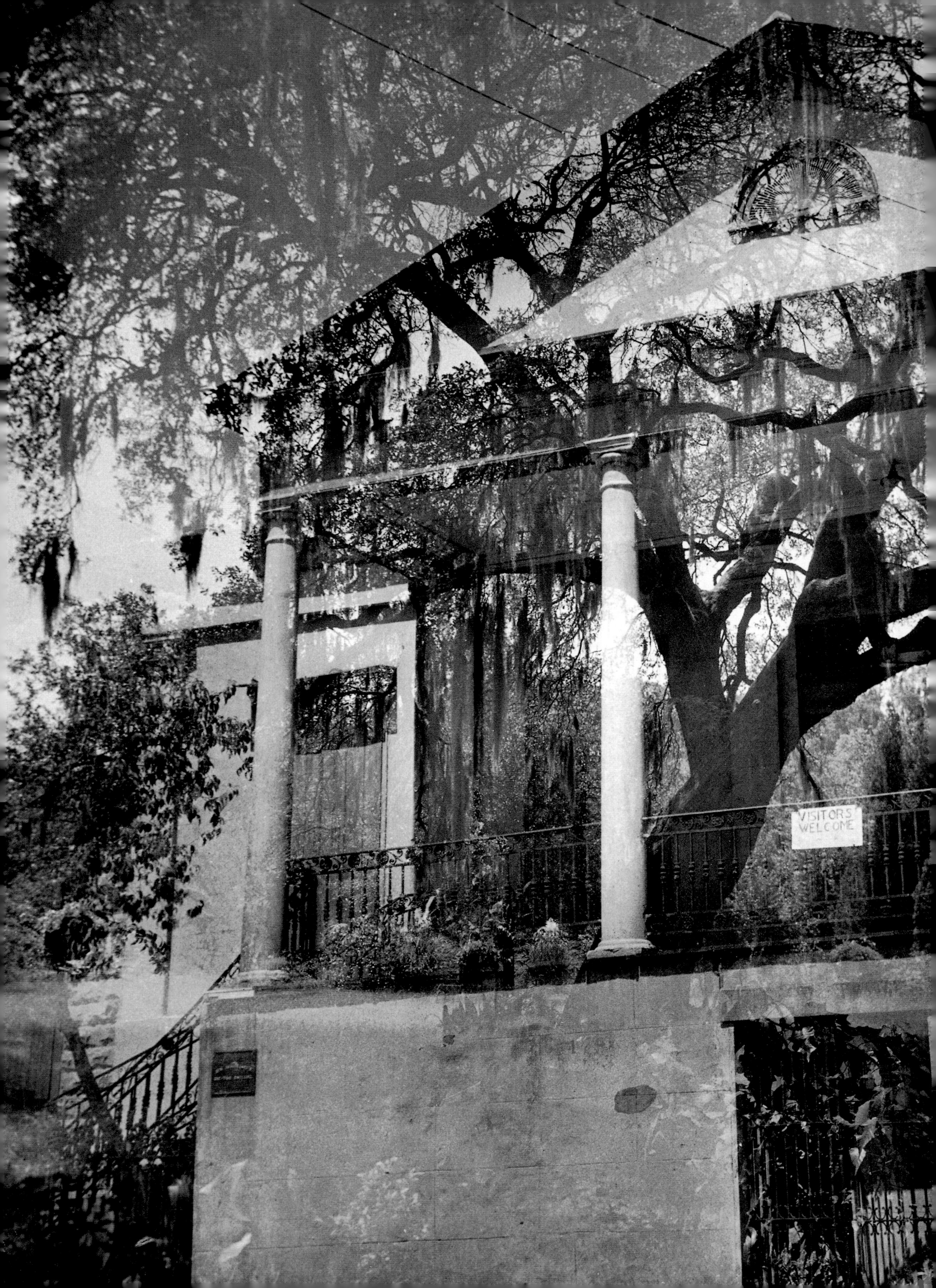
VISITORS
WELCOME

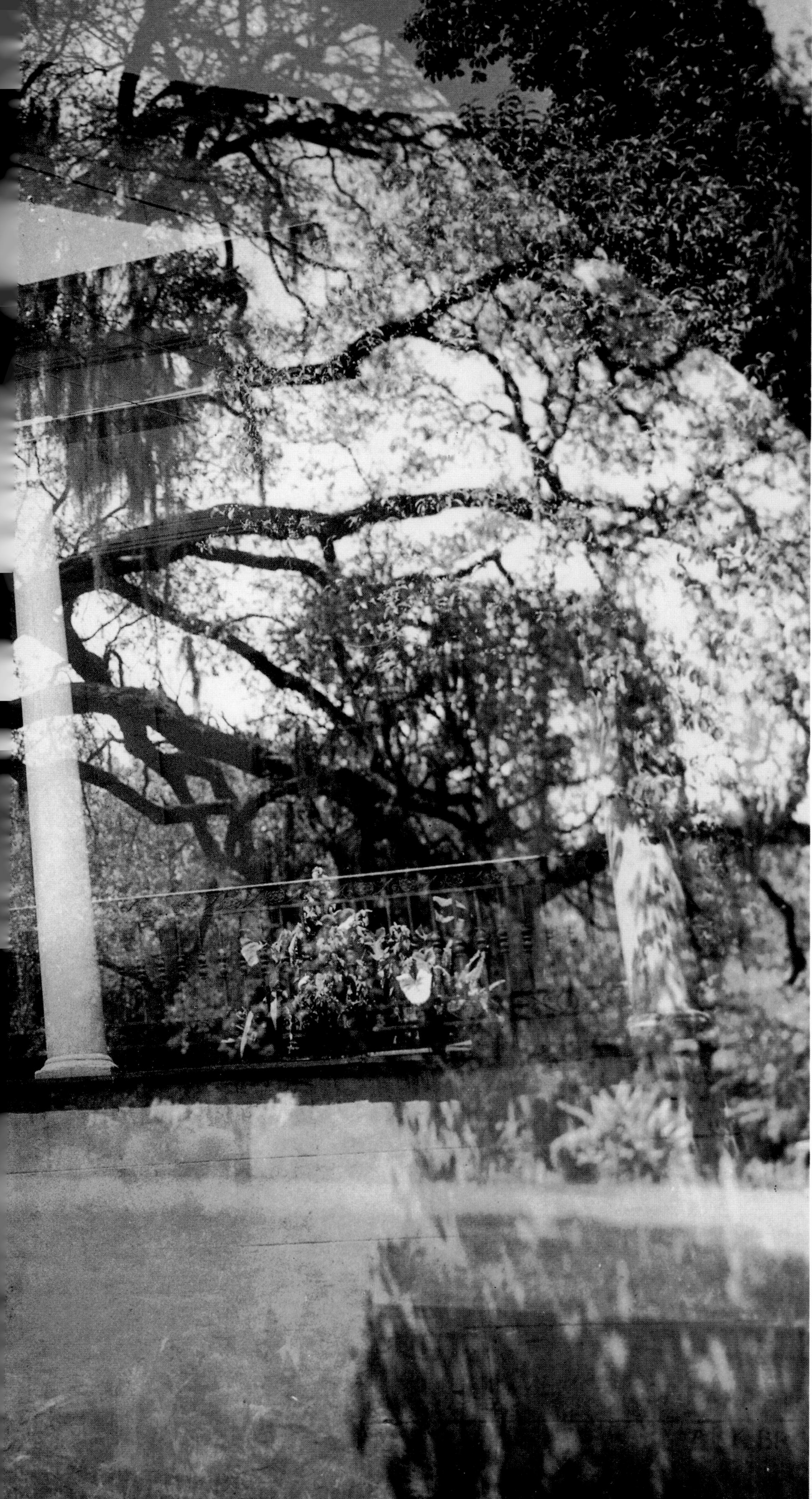

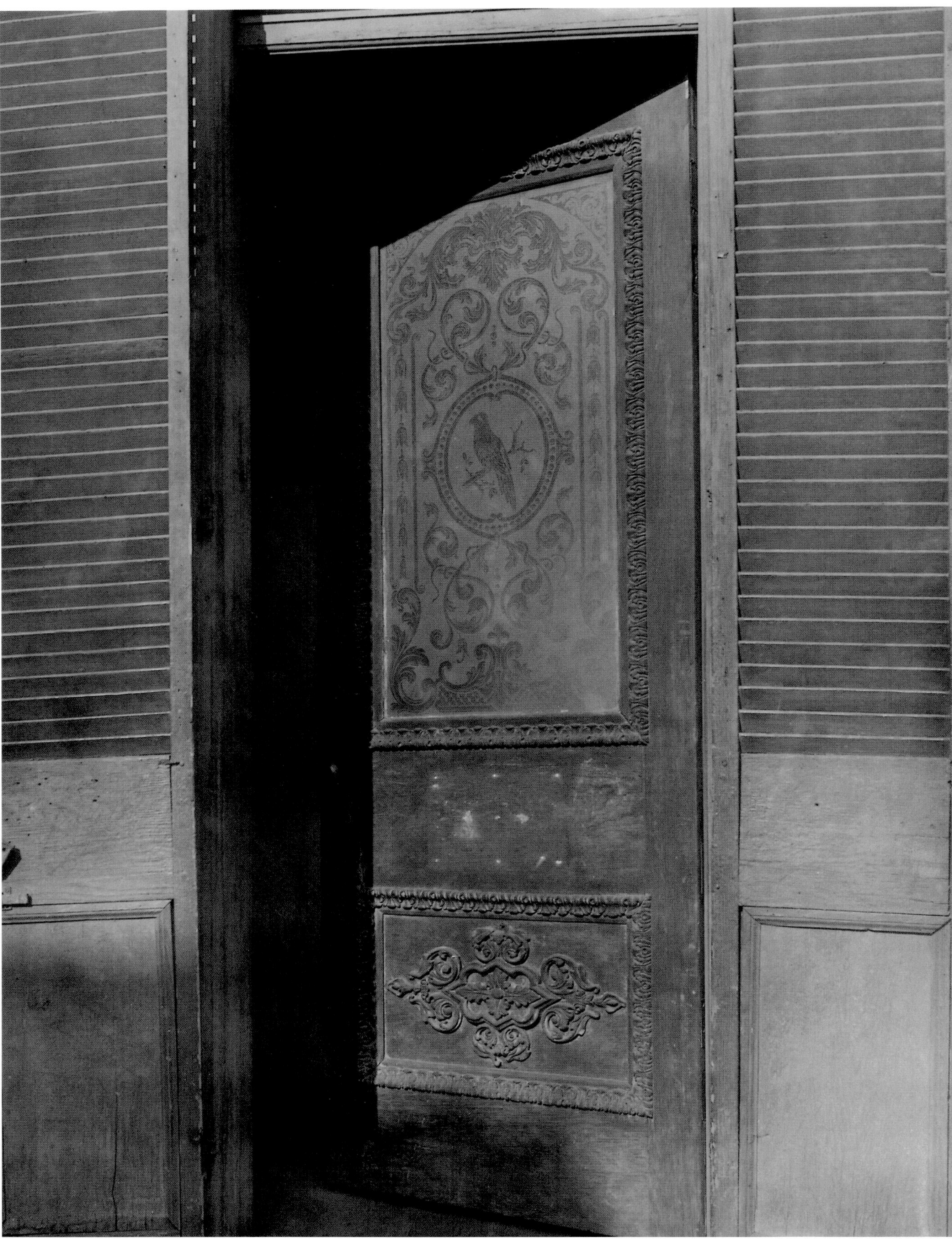

APPENDIX: CLARENCE JOHN LAUGHLIN'S DESCRIPTIONS OF HIS PHOTOGRAPHIC GROUPS

GROUP A: STILL LIFES

This group, the earliest on which I worked, was begun in 1935. I started with no formal training at all as a painter or photographer, but with some background as a writer, and a vast background as a reader. Although this group originated in a desire to develop further an interest in composition (incited by the discovery of certain art magazines in the 1930s) it eventually became involved in an urge to see how far my feelings about objects could become projected through the camera; and in the discovery of objects which could become the clues to changes in the nature of American culture. Thus, here, as in much of my work, there is a progression from the semi-abstract to the poetic.

GROUP B: MARINE FORMS

Though ships, originally, formed most of the material for this group — the photographer's attention, later, focused chiefly on objects involved with the mystery of the sea — and on the kind of "hyperreality" which the camera, alone, can create . . .

GROUP C: TREE FORMS

This Group began in 1937; but much work was added to it from 1946 through 1960. Its emphasis was not so much on the beauty of natural forms in themselves, as on the mysterious realm where natural forms intermingle significantly and strangely with projections from the mind of man. This realm is related to the great and ancient kingdom of fantasy which forms the core of all the arts, and which extends in painting from Hieronymus Bosch through James Ensor and Alfred Kubin to come down in our own time to Paul Klee. Therefore in this group the trees become something more than trees — they become involved with the child's sense of wonder, and they become clues also to the special and personal associations with which we invest all objects. And thus the photographer, like the painter, is seen to be able, when approaching nature, to convey something of his own inner world while, at the same time, evoking some of the ambiance of mystery which surrounds all things, despite all our pretentious "knowledge."

GROUP D: EARLY INDUSTRIALISM

This group presents images of the gradual and confused impact of industrialism in the deep south.

Opposite:
DOOR OF THE PARROT, NUMBER ONE
1941

Weeks Hall to Clarence John Laughlin, November 23, 1939

You have no idea how I enjoyed seeing my kind of New Orleans in such a form that it can be taken out and looked at without the interruption of having to go there.

GROUP E: METAL MAGIC

This group also saw its inception in 1936. It is concerned, in photographic terms, with the magnificence of steel, the strange and menacing magic of the contemporary world of metal forms — the amazing crystallizations of man's will and man's greed, in the objects of industry.

GROUP F: GLASS MAGIC

Glass is fascinating because it acts so variably and subtly with light: offers so may suggestions that so-called reality is not the simple thing we usually conceive it to be: that reality embodies many planes and many kinds of meanings. Too, it does many surprising things with space; and this group, begun in 1938, gives examples of this and, in addition, attempts to push further the magic quality which Eugène Atget, the amazing old French photographer, obtained in his photographs of shop windows of nineteenth-century Paris — pictures in which he went well beyond his own documentary approach.

GROUP G: FANTASY IN OLD NEW ORLEANS

This group, which is quite large, deals with the special and indigenous fantasy which appeared in many New Orleans buildings, and which is found in nearly all of the stone and iron forms of the New Orleans cemeteries. Nineteenth-century New Orleans had a physical and psychological background unlike that of any other American city. This special kind of fantasy appeared at one end of the scale in the unparalleled development of funereal art in the old burial grounds of the city; and at the other end of the scale (as a counterbalance, perhaps), in the wild fantasy of the Mardi Gras.

GROUP H: LOST NEW ORLEANS

In this very extensive group of pictures, begun in 1937, I attempted to isolate visually the authentic quality of the old buildings of New Orleans — those buildings which had neither been prettified for the tourist trade nor "renovated" for commerce: of those streets in New Orleans which were "lost" in time. The buildings were approached as psychological and poetic documents, rather than from the more narrow viewpoints of the historian and the architect.

GROUP I: SATIRES

Most photographers have never, except in a very superficial way, extensively used the camera's intrinsic ability to create biting satire against a society filled with many forms of hypocrisy and with countless forms of social injustice. But the very significant German photographer Hans Herzfelde (or John Heartfield) conclusively showed, during Hitler's rise to power, the camera's great capacities in this direction. My own efforts in this field are involved either with carefully arranged effects which attempt to transcend mere "contrivance"; or else exploit the accidental sardonic juxtaposition of objects.

GROUP J: THE IMAGES OF THE LOST

Group J deals with the people rejected by our society; it is the first group primarily devoted to human beings. But the people were very seldom photographed where they were actually found. Instead, a difficult method was used: a special background was selected for each person (often from places discovered previously) with the intention of making the background work, not only in terms of design, but in terms of a subtle revelation of the overall social situation of the person. The people themselves were not used as models — they were not posed — nor were they used as "sociological documents." The attempt was to treat them as individual human beings. The overall composition was determined carefully on the ground glass. But the exposure was not made till each person seemed to reveal himself by some spontaneous gesture or expression.

GROUP K: VISUAL POEMS

In 1940 I tried to push further the integration of the human figure with especially selected backgrounds which I had to some degree begun in "Group I: Satires" and "Group J: The Images of the Lost"; except that here the integration was not in terms of satiric intent, or of social revelation, but rather in terms of poetic concepts.

Many of these pictures are examples of the interaction of photography and literature, using either carefully arranged whole figures, or highly individualized portrait effects in close-up; but always with poetic emphasis. Some of the pictures started as literary concepts; for many years before I began photography I had been a voracious reader, and in about 1925 had begun to write. Many of the figures in this group create combinations of line and tone and mood possible only in photography, and show how the camera can evoke hidden elements in human beings as surely as does painting.

GROUP L: POEMS OF THE INTERIOR WORLD

I feel that this group represents my most original and difficult project up to this time. In it I tried to create a mythology from our contemporary world. This mythology, instead of having gods and goddesses — has the personifications of our fears and frustrations, our desires and dilemmas. By means of a complex integration of human figures (never presented as individuals, since the figures are intended only as symbols of states of mind); carefully chosen backgrounds; and selected objects, I attempted to project the symbolic reality of our time, so that the pictures become images of the psychological substructure of confusion, want, and fear which have led to the two great wars, and which may lead to the end of human society. Fear and desire have the deepest roots in us, and in the modern world their forms have become peculiarly sharpened and twisted. In releasing the symbolic contents of objects my intent was to present settings for the drama of the misery and madness of our time; to deal with the depersonalization of man, and the conditions leading to the rise of the authoritarian ideologies. But the pictures were not conceived in a coldly conscious way. They were arrived at mostly by means of subconscious intuitions and compulsions; and thus they have a number of different levels of meaning. All this, in 1939, when this group was initiated, represented a new departure for American photography. Even now, in this country, the ability of the camera to deal with psychological reality, and to evoke symbols, has scarcely been touched. For those not interested in symbolism, these pictures can be seen in terms of their basic level of meaning, which is design in terms of light and dark. For those interested, a more complete discussion of the character and objective of this group can be found in *Poet's Gallery Series* magazine, no. 2 — a poetry magazine published by Harper Square Press, Chicago, 1968 — where a number of pictures from this series are also reproduced.

GROUP M: THE LOUISIANA PLANTATIONS

Group M deals with the architectural achievements of the last great nonurban culture of this country — the nineteenth-century plantation culture of the lower Mississippi Valley. But this is not entirely in terms of architectural recording, since it includes a number of pictures dealing with the atmosphere of houses, and with the poetry and the enigma of time in these structures from the past. Also, there are two subsections in this group; one dealing with the Negro country churches and the other with the swamp burial grounds where is found an extraordinary kind of folk art. The primary objectives of Group M are: (1) to outline the evolution of Louisiana plantation architecture from its origins under strong French provincial influence in the eighteenth century — to the onset of the Civil War; (2) to indicate how in the 1830s and 1840s a truly indigenous type of house appeared on the Louisiana plantation, which was unlike anything else in America, or in Europe, where the plan of the house grew out of the nature of the climate and of the materials.

Within this century, fire and flood, levee set-backs, the ravages of heat and dampness, and the neglect due to impoverishment, have all taken an increasing toll of the houses left from the great nineteenth-century efflorescence. Working against the accelerating tide of destruction, during the years 1939 to 1941, and 1946 to 1953, I tried to rescue some of the tragic and poetic beauty of this architecture. Some of the more than 2,000 negatives resulting appeared in my second book, *Ghosts Along the Mississippi*, with about 50,000 words of text.

GROUP N: FORMS OF TODAY

[This group consists primarily of buildings constructed after World War II, usually photographed on assignment for the architect or contractor.]

GROUP O: COLOR EXPERIMENTS

Since I believe that there are a great many more relationships between painting and photography than are recognized, or accepted, and since I further believe that these relationships do not necessarily involve the mere copying of one medium by the other, I have devoted some time to exploring the borderland between these two arts, primarily during the period 1943 to 1946 — the only time when the facilities for such exploration were available to me.

I evolved a number of techniques to accomplish this exploration: such as the use of watercolor and oil on photographic collages; the use of photographic dyes and ink on photograms; the use of photographic dyes and inks directly on mordanted paper (with or without a photographic image); also the use of wash-off relief images on mordanted paper, but in unorthodox ways.

For some of these techniques I do not have names. But enough has been clearly done to indicate that all the technical discoveries in color photographic chemistry, etc., have esthetic potentialities which, as yet, have scarcely been touched.

GROUP P: ROCK FORMS

Since all the material in this small group was photographed in the west — and since the treatment of such material by such photographers as Ansel Adams has become so familiar and accepted — there was a strong temptation for the photographer to fall into the "Purist" approach.

A study of the pictures, however, should indicate that the photographer varies the character of his approach in accordance with what the nature of the subject matter suggests to his imagination. He has never tried to force one method of approach on every kind of material. He has always attempted to make these alterations in the use of the camera — subject, in turn, to the overall guidance of a personal vision.

So, even in this group, where it would have been so easy to use the accepted approach — he tried to do something more subtle; to incorporate "Purism" merely as a basis upon which to build his own special animistic and poetic vision — and thus project, through the material, meanings which "Purism" would not have been capable of.

GROUP Q: NEW ANATOMIES

In this comparatively small group, which began in 1951, I have tried to show that the camera can explore the plastic potentialities of the human body in just as real a sense as, for instance, Picasso has done in some marvelous drawings where he makes use of numerous kinds of distortion in recreating the body; although in these photos distortion is not the method actually used. Nevertheless we are presented with visions of the body which it would be impossible for the physical eye directly to see. The pictures go completely beyond the kind of "recording" function usually assigned to the camera, and instead of giving us the results of direct vision, give us far more — the hyper-real vision created by the inner eye in man — the poetic, desiring, and dreaming eye. Because of this, the erotic element becomes all the more intense. But due to the puritanical code dominating this country till recently, none of these pictures have ever been published or exhibited before. The basic quotation for this series is from Hart Crane: "New thresholds, new anatomies!" And the last half of this quotation is, literally, the subject for this group.

GROUP R: SCULPTURE SEEN ANEW

This group is devoted to showing significant sculpture — from all periods, and from all over the world. But the selections were made entirely from American collections, public and private. Because of the richness of American collections, and since there are over 1,700 negatives, the group eventually became a sort of visual outline of world sculpture.

The other main purpose of the group is to outline some of the methods (and there are quite a variety of such methods developed in these pictures) by which the camera can be used to interpret sculpture — to intensify the experience of sculpture beyond the direct experience of the physical eye.

The photographer has designed a very large show entitled "The Bronze Age to Brancusi" — based on these pictures. The show consists of over 700 images, on 105 panels, and opened up in the Detroit Institute of Arts in March 1957.

GROUP S: THE MAGIC OF THE OBJECT

It should be pointed out that Group S is the only one of the many groups I worked on which is entirely devoted to so-called commonplace objects. In this group I try to show how the photographer, like the painter and poet, can release a level of meaning from the most ordinary objects, which has nothing to do with their naturalistic meaning. The photographer, of course, does this through intensely personal vision (just as is true of the painter and the poet) and when this happens, what the photographer is really dealing with is what the human mind has projected into the object: the secret language of inanimate objects, the hidden images of man's hopes and joys, his dreams and desires, by which he makes more human the inhuman world around him. Although most of these pictures use the "found" object, all the objects are, in a deeper sense, "arranged," that is, lighting, composition, and other factors have been used, both consciously and compulsively, to make more manifest the hidden meanings these objects have for the sensibility of the photographer. But, aside from all this, many of the objects in these pictures can be truly considered part of the iconography of our time.

GROUP T: THE MYSTERY OF SPACE

This group is involved in showing how the photographer can deal with space problems in as real a sense as the painter, but without the help of color: how, for instance, the camera can collapse space (i.e., make a three-dimensional object look flat); or multiply space (i.e., make a two-dimensional object look three-dimensional). Also, this group indicates how the camera can semi-abstract objects; and create significant space illusions, as well, by exploiting the difference between physical space and visual space.

GROUP U: AMERICAN VICTORIAN ARCHITECTURE

Over 5,000 sheet film negatives were made for this group over a period of twenty years. The pictures were made in such cities as Chicago, Milwaukee, St.

Louis, Memphis, Little Rock, Salt Lake City, San Francisco, Los Angeles, Galveston, and San Antonio, and many of the pictures are involved with the special feeling of certain houses and with the spirit of American places. Among the objectives of this group were (1) to show that the 1880s and 90s were probably the most important period architecturally in American cultural history; (2) to show why a new evaluation of American Victorian buildings must be made; (3) to discover important new architectural material from this period, not in the books; (4) to show that the American Victorians had made some very important discoveries, mostly by intuition, in the highly significant field which can be called "psychological functionalism" — which enabled them to understand the supremely important roles of fantasy and decoration in architecture — in a manner far beyond anything we are capable of; and led to many of their houses being far more human and livable than ours; (5) to show that it was little-known Victorian architects who first broke with European architectural traditions, rather than such people as Sullivan and Wright.

GROUP V: VINTAGE PRINTS

[This group of varied material contains the very early work of the photographer. Many of these pictures were subsequently assigned to other groups.]

GROUP W: FANTASY IN EUROPE

Even in Europe, just as in the United States, the late nineteenth century seems the period most ignored. So when I reached Paris for the first time in October 1965, and realized the incredible riches of photography that could easily be found on almost every street, and also realized my limited time, I quickly determined to restrict myself to the 1880s and 90s. It was in this that I discovered my roots; it is this period which is closest to my heart; because it is this period which was the most deeply involved with the tremendous importance of the fantastic in human lives, and the primacy of the needs of the human imagination. And, of course, as always, but especially here, I found more material than I could possibly cope with; so that I ran out of both time and money. But I hope to go back, and, ultimately, to do a large show on this marvelous city, whose streets have nurtured so many poets, whose atmosphere is the mother of the creative spirit.

In time I also managed to get to England, where I was fortunate enough to be able to do a set of pictures of the peerless Brighton Pavilion.

[N.B. Descriptions for Groups N and V in brackets were supplied by the Historic New Orleans Collection.]

AUTHOR BIOGRAPHIES

Andrei Codrescu was born in Romania in 1946. Since emigrating to the United States in 1966, he has published poetry, memoirs, fiction, and essays. He is a regular commentator on National Public Radio and has written and starred in the Peabody Award–winning movie *Road Scholar*. He teaches writing at Louisiana State University and edits the journal *Exquisite Corpse*. His latest books are *The Dog with the Chip in His Neck* and *Alien Candor: Selected Poems, 1970–1996*.

Albert Belisle Davis, novelist in residence at Nicholls State University in Thibodaux, Louisiana, is the fiction editor for the *Louisiana English Journal*. The author of two novels published by Louisiana State University Press, *Leechtime* (1989) and *Marquis at Bay* (1992), he is currently writing his third novel.

Ellen Gilchrist, a former New Orleanian now living in Fayetteville, Arkansas, is the author of fourteen books of poetry, fiction, and essays, including *In the Land of Dreamy Dreams* and *Net of Jewels*. She is the winner of the National Book Award for Fiction for *Victory Over Japan* and has received numerous other awards. Her latest book is *Sarah Conley*.

Shirley Ann Grau was born in Louisiana, spent her childhood in Alabama, and now lives in Houston. She is the author of six novels — *The Hard Blue Sky, The House on Coliseum Street, The Keepers of the House* (awarded the Pulitzer Prize for fiction), *The Condor Passes, Evidence of Love,* and *Roadwalkers* — and three collections of stories: *The Black Prince, The Wind Shifting West,* and *Nine Women*.

Jon Kukla is director of the Historic New Orleans Collection. An authority on early Southern political and intellectual history, he earned his Ph.D. from the University of Toronto in 1980. His wide-ranging interests are reflected in books, essays, and reviews on subjects as varied as architectural history, disease, cooking, and Anglo-American poetry. He is currently writing about the Louisiana Purchase and the second half of American history.

John H. Lawrence, director of museum programs at the Historic New Orleans Collection, is a photographic historian/critic and photographer. He is associate editor of the *New Orleans Art Review* and writes and lectures frequently on photographic subjects, both historical and contemporary. He has written a guide to the Collection's photographic holdings and *Preservation Guide 2: Photographs*.

Jonathan Williams, who lives on a mountain in western North Carolina, considers himself "the Jesse Helms of American poetry — mean as a snake and twice as tenacious." Having published poems and essays, published *The Jargon Society,* and photographed for forty-five years since attending Black Mountain College, he takes comfort in now being "internationally unknown." It takes a Clarence Laughlin to ferret him out, and there have never been many of those about.

John Wood holds professorships in both the departments of art and English at McNeese State University in Lake Charles, Louisiana. He is the author of three books of poetry and six books of art criticism and was cocurator of the 1995 Smithsonian Institution exhibition *Secrets of the Dark Chamber*. His books have won the Iowa Poetry Prize twice, the American Photographic Historical Society's Outstanding Book of the Year Award, *Choice*'s Outstanding Academic Books of 1992, and the *New York Review of Books* Best Books of 1995.

ACKNOWLEDGMENTS

Clarence John Laughlin transferred his massive career archive to the Historic New Orleans Collection in 1981. Since then, many staff members have contributed to the processing and care of some forty thousand master prints, working photographs, and negatives, as well as boxes of manuscripts and other artifacts that document a life of genius. As befits a large and important collection, countless staff have worked with the Laughlin material and thereby contributed to this book in one way or another over the past sixteen years.

For their steadfast support of these efforts, we are grateful to president Mary Louise Christovich and the board of the Kemper and Leila Williams Foundation: G. Henry Pierson, Jr., John E. Williams, Fred M. Smith, and Suzanne T. Mestayer.

John H. Lawrence, then curator of photography, championed the acquisition of the Laughlin collection and — with support from the late Benjamin Yancey and former directors Dode Platou and Stanton M. Frazar — guided negotiations to a successful conclusion. Special thanks must be extended to Jude Solomon for her role in organizing Laughlin's photographs for publication and exhibition, and to photographers Jan White Brantley and Elizabeth Kellner for top-quality advice and assistance despite impossible deadlines.

Susan Larson, the able book review editor of the *New Orleans Times-Picayune*, offered many rounds of well-informed counsel. Her love of Laughlin's work gave special authority to her advice about which authors to commission for the essays, and we are grateful to Andrei Codrescu, Albert Belisle Davis, Ellen Gilchrist, Shirley Ann Grau, Jonathan Williams, and John Wood for eloquently responding to Laughlin's muse.

Haunter of Ruins reflects the vision and hard work of Patricia Brady and John H. Lawrence, and painstaking editorial and production work by Karen Dane, Ken Wong, and their colleagues at Bulfinch Press. To these and other friends, our hearty thanks for joining in this appreciation of the multifaceted genius of Clarence John Laughlin.

Jon Kukla
Director, The Historic New Orleans Collection

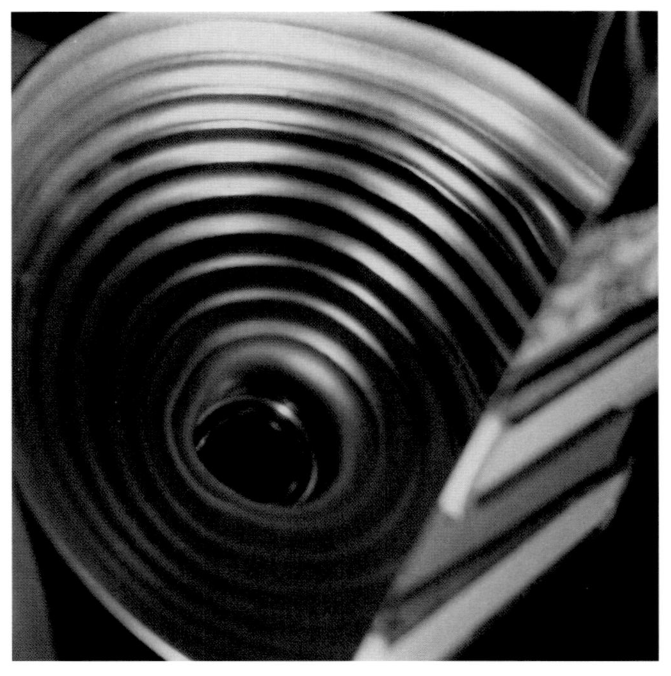

WOMAN REFLECTED IN A MIRROR 1938 (DETAIL)

DESIGNED BY SUSAN MARSH

TYPE SET IN COCHIN AND FUTURA

PRINTED BY STAMPERIA VALDONEGA, VERONA, ITALY